The Challenge *of the* Lord's Prayer

A phrase-by-phrase reflection on
the prayer Jesus taught us

John Cox

**kevin
mayhew**

kevin
mayhew

First published in Great Britain in 2017 by Kevin Mayhew Ltd
Buxhall, Stowmarket, Suffolk IP14 3BW
Tel: +44 (0) 1449 737978 Fax: +44 (0) 1449 737834
E-mail: info@kevinmayhew.com

www.kevinmayhew.com

9 8 7 6 5 4 3 2 1 0

ISBN 978 1 84867 906 1
Catalogue No. 1501546

Cover design by Rob Mortonson
© Image used under licence from Shutterstock Inc.
Edited by Nicki Copeland
Typeset by Angela Selfe

Printed and bound in Great Britain

Contents

9. And Lead Us Not Into Temptation

10. But Deliver Us From Evil

About the author

Having spent rather a long time at various universities including Cambridge, Oxford and the University College of Rhodesia and Nyasaland, John was ordained to a curacy in the diocese of Liverpool in 1968. He spent a second curacy in an inner-city ex-slum parish in Birmingham and became rector in the same parish. After a five-year period at Church House, Westminster where he was Senior Selection Secretary, helping to select ordinands, he was made Canon Treasurer at Southwark Cathedral and Diocesan Director of Ordinands and Post-ordination training.

Following four years as Vicar of Roehampton he moved to become Archdeacon of Sudbury in the Diocese of St Edmundsbury and Ipswich in 1995. When he retired in 2006 he was asked to be the part-time Diocesan Director of Education, a job he did for nearly four and a half years before retiring for a second time. It has been during these retirement years that John has been writing for Kevin Mayhew, in between being chair of governors at a primary academy, playing golf and enjoying river cruises.

For details of all John Cox's books, please visit our website: www.kevinmayhew.com

Introduction
JESUS AND PRAYER

The Lord's Prayer must be one of the most widely known of all prayers. Even these days it is still learnt by heart in many schools. There are sung versions, signed versions, danced versions. It is part of almost all church services, and congregations repeat it in one form or another every Sunday. So why have a book about it? We all say it often enough. What more is there to be said about it?

Well, we may say it, but that's not quite the same as knowing it, knowing its meaning, facing its challenges as well as finding it a comfort. Even its meaning is not quite as obvious as we might think.

We normally have the prayer only in translation, of course, both in various versions of the Bible and in prayer books. And translations inevitably have an element of interpretation about them. There is not always just one meaning to the original words, and translators have to make choices – choices that can make a difference to how we understand exactly what it was that Jesus was saying. The meaning is also dependent to some extent upon the context in which it was originally said, the context in which it was remembered and recorded in the Gospels (in Matthew and Luke), and the context in which we say the prayer today.

Jesus believed he was bringing in the kingdom of God, God's new age. He and the early Church believed they were living in the Last Days, and this inevitably coloured many of the things they said. We don't have that same immediate expectation as they did. The Last Days feel as though they are a long time coming, and that stretching of the timescale makes a difference. Our concern about temptation and evil is more immediate and less related to what will happen at the end of time.

None of this means that the Lord's Prayer is not relevant today. It is properly 'ageless'.

We sometimes think that prayer is all about asking, and the Lord's Prayer certainly has requests in it – for 'daily bread', that we will be forgiven, that we will not be led into temptation and that we will be delivered from evil. But in asking for things for ourselves, our very asking also challenges us about what we are doing – in relation to God and in relation to others. We ask that our needs are met, but how far do we go in helping to meet the needs of the hungry and homeless? We want to be forgiven, but how forgiving are we? We look to be released from what is evil in our world and in our hearts, but how concerned are we about the evil injustices of our world that keep people oppressed and deprived? And before Jesus encourages us to ask for things for ourselves, he ensures that we first acknowledge the honour and holiness of our heavenly Father. There is much to be considered in this brief prayer that Jesus gave us, much to learn for our spiritual growth.

The Lord's Prayer is not all that Jesus said on the topic of prayer. He spent a considerable time in prayer – formally in the synagogue and privately out on the hills. It was a vital aspect of his relationship with his Father, and in his role as a rabbi, the disciples and others would have looked to him to teach them about prayer.

Jesus didn't go in for long prayers or for a great show in praying. He suggested it was better to say our prayers in private and without rambling on and on (Matthew 6:5-8). Better to come to God humbly confessing one's faults than boasting of one's good deeds (Luke 18:9-14). If you have a need, just ask (Luke 11:9; John 14:14), and be persistent in prayer (Luke 18:2-7). Prayer can be demanding, as Jesus found in the Garden of Gethsemane. For prayer is ultimately all about a relationship. It is one of the ways we discover what it is God asks of us as well as what God has to offer us. There may well be times that, like Jesus, we ask for what is demanded of us to be removed, but if we follow Jesus' example, our final word must be the same as his: 'Yet, not what I want, but what you want' (Mark 14:36).

If we would learn from Jesus how to pray we need to listen to his teaching, follow his example and pray the prayer he taught us.

Just a word about how the book is set out. It considers the Lord's Prayer phrase by phrase, looking at the meaning both for Jesus and for us, what it tells us about God and the challenge it presents to us.

Each chapter has two parts. In Part A, the focus is on the meaning of the phrase being considered, with a discussion of issues raised by the original text and by translations. The emphasis is upon information and the implications for the Christian understanding of God and for living out that understanding. Part B is more of a dialogue between the author and the reader. Readers are encouraged to spend time reflecting upon the points raised in the earlier part of the chapter and to consider how that might affect the way they pray.

ONE

Our . . .

PART A
Individuality

Since the 1960s, American social demographers and market researchers have used letters to identify members of successive generations. Following the baby boomers of the 1950s and 1960s, 1966–1976 saw the arrival of Generation X. Typically, they were the latchkey generation often exposed to divorce and childcare. Better educated than previous generations, they were largely sceptical and less often exercised the right to a vote. They have been succeeded by Generations Y and now Z.

Personally, and with only observation and subjective viewpoint to back it up, I think this has been the time of the 'I' generations. There has been a growing emphasis on the individual, of personal choice, on what matters to me. My opinion and my happiness are what count. There is a scepticism about authority. While social media can be viewed as individuals making use of modern technology to break out of isolation, much of it actually looks like individual indulgence scattered to the world. The 'blame society' has emerged from, and has itself encouraged, an emphasis on my rights rather than my responsibilities. We seem a long way from the days of J. F. Kennedy's inaugural speech in 1961 when he famously said, 'Ask not what your country can do for you, but what you can do for your country'. Salman Rushdie in an interview on *World at One* suggested that the increasing individualism is making us less appreciative and less open to wider social contacts where difference brings richness of experience.[1] The groups we relate to are narrowing to simply those who are like us.

---

1. *World at One*, BBC Radio, 30 May 2016.

It is easy to exaggerate, and any attempt to characterise a generation can ignore alternative evidence. Eating out appears to be on the increase. Record amounts of money are raised by charity events such as Comic Relief. There isn't unmitigated selfishness. But among the elderly in particular, isolation is a widespread problem. Youngsters are increasingly prone to stress and mental illness and appear to have less emotional resilience than previous generations. Among teenagers, rates of depression and anxiety have risen by 70 per cent over the past 25 years.[2]

We are, of course, social animals, and basically remain so. In the past, social interaction was necessary for survival, and isolated individuals had the odds stacked against them. Membership of such groups as the family, the clan or the tribe was very significant and shaped the way people felt about their personal identity. Big ideas, such as a religious faith, provided the social glue for allegiances wider than these groupings and extended them beyond national borders.

The individual and the corporate

For human beings, the interplay of the individual and the group is more complex than in much of the animal and plant world where the continuation of the species takes precedence over the needs of the individual. We are more conscious and self-conscious of our individuality and of the individual's rights. Different political systems manage this balance differently, but even in a free democracy like that in Britain there can still be fears of the State being too much of a Nanny on the one hand and a Big Brother on the other. Pressure groups such as Liberty seek to ensure that individual rights are not trampled on by the demands of the political/social system. In dictatorships, of course, such action is viewed as dangerous and seditious.

There is the same interplay or tension within religious experience. As we said above, religion has been one of the major forces in ensuring large

---

2. Young Minds offers information and statistics about young people's mental health. Available at www.youngminds.org.uk (last accessed 5 December 2016).

social allegiances. One only has to think of the way the major religions of the world have an international membership and have contributed both in the past and still today to the establishment of empires that stretch far beyond national boundaries and specific cultures. Religious belief has the power to hold people together in a common mindset so that the individual has a level of commonality with peoples from all over the world. When the differences among the members become too marked, there is the creation of sects. The mainstream orthodoxy can react violently in the attempt to maintain solidarity. Individuals are declared heretics and groups 'excommunicated'. At its worst, it leads to religious wars where the demands of religion linked with political power seek to preserve or enlarge the influence of the dominant group. We saw this in Europe with the religious wars of the sixteenth and seventeenth centuries and are seeing it today with the rise of the so-called Islamic State and its declared aim to create a worldwide Islamic caliphate based on a particular understanding of Islam.

At the more personal level of religious believing there is also a degree of possible tension between the individual and the corporate. In broad terms, it might be said that the Catholic Church has emphasised the corporate while the Protestant churches have emphasised the individual. But of course it is a matter of balance rather than being an absolute. For the Catholic Church there is an emphasis upon the Church's teaching, the tradition of the Church, the way the Church has interpreted Scripture. For the Protestants the individual's personal act of faith commitment to Christ has been of particular importance.

These differences have shaped the way the denominations have seen such matters as what is necessary for salvation, the nature of sacraments, the way of relating to God and the role of the clergy. However important individual personal faith is, it is generally recognised that being part of a worshipping fellowship is also important for faith to grow and be maintained. This has been formalised in the expectations set out in days of obligation or through other attendance requirements. A single piece of coal soon burns out, but coals together sustain a fire. For faith to be nurtured, for worshippers to be cared for, for mission and community action, Christians need one another. Social contact is a significant part of what people value about going to church, and the provision of coffee and biscuits after services bears witness to this.

At the same time, the value and worth of every individual is a central tenet of the Christian understanding of what it is to be human and of the way we should treat one another. It is based on the understanding that God cares for each one of us and knows each one of us intimately – even to the point that the number of hairs on my head is known to God! (Matthew 10:30). As a child of God, each person is of infinite worth. The forgiveness of God, with its sacrificial cost as shown on the cross, is for each individual as well as for the world (John 3:16). Loved in this way by the Father, Christians are called to love others with the same infinite concern for them as for individuals. And that, of course, is not always easy. As Charlie Brown once confessed, 'I love mankind. It's people I can't stand.'

The bond with Jesus and with others

When Jesus began his exemplar prayer he started with 'Our . . .', not with 'My . . .'. This was not because he wished to deny the importance of an individual's personal approach to God or relationship with God. In John's Gospel, he often referred to God as 'my Father' (for example, John 14:18-24). By beginning his prayer with 'Our' he was emphasising two important bonds: the bond between himself and his followers, and the bond between his followers. The relationship he had with the Father, although in some sense unique, was a relationship his followers could share. It was open to them as well. When we say 'Our' we are joining with Jesus in addressing the God he called Father. But in approaching and addressing God, we do it also as those who acknowledge that others, indeed all people, have the same opportunity to approach God in this way. The relationship with God is not a private, individual possession – it is something we share with Christ and with others.

Over the years there have been different ways of beginning statements of faith. Some have started, 'I believe . . .' and others, 'We believe . . .'

Each has its own significance. 'I believe . . .' emphasises that this faith is not just something others have but that it is what I believe, hold on to, am committed to. But it is also a belief that is shared with others, something that together we can make our assent to, and so it is good that there are forms that reflect this: 'We believe . . .' Personal faith can go through rocky times, and to affirm every line of a creed with integrity might be difficult. But being part of a fellowship where members together hold these beliefs is both a support and an encouragement. It is right that when we worship together we should affirm our faith with 'We believe . . .'. There is a bond of faith as well as fellowship.

Jesus envisaged his followers praying together as well as individually in the privacy of a closed room. At such times they bring their requests, their confessions, their thanks to God together. Their praying starts with 'Our . . .'. Even on one's own it can sometimes be very important to know that one is not in fact alone; that in our praying we are joining with others, countless numbers of them across the world. We do not have to feel isolated when we pray, for no matter what time of the day or night, there are always those who are joining in the prayer, 'our' prayer.

Jesus' prayer reflects the inclusive nature of our humanity. The 'our' in this sense has no boundaries. God is not my possession and nor is he the possession of the group I most immediately identify with. No one, no group, no church, no nation has exclusive rights to God. Prayer to him is not restricted to particular groups on the basis of age or race or gender or orientation or status. It is not restricted even by religion. The 'our' is all inclusive. That's how God sees it. That's how Jesus saw it. We don't always see it that way.

PART B

The prayer group I belonged to at college always sat in a circle. There were obvious good reasons for that. At the start of the meeting there would normally be an opportunity to share items for thanksgiving and matters of concern. We would then move to a time of prayer in which each person took their turn to offer a prayer. No matter where I sat in the circle I always seemed to end up being the last one to pray, by which time all the things we had previously talked about had been mentioned. It may have contributed to my feeling less than comfortable when praying in such a setting.

Praying alone and together

Many people, of course, feel at ease no matter what the setting – be it in a prayer meeting, in an act of worship, at home privately. But not everyone. That may be true for you. For some, the formality of a set liturgy and led intercessions can feel rather stuffy and restricting, while for others it provides a structure into within which they feel a freedom to enter without having to worry about the words. Some feel most at ease in the privacy of their home, talking and listening to God with the naturalness of conversing with a friend. Still others find themselves tongue-tied, unsure what to do and what to say and feeling that the resulting silence is embarrassing. We are all different, and whatever is true for us we need to remember that God is always listening, as we say, 'more ready to hear than we are to speak'.

Do you find you are more comfortable in one setting rather than another? Why do you think this is so? Does it matter?

The fellowship of others in a time of prayer can be very encouraging and supportive, even if we ourselves never open our mouth. By beginning his prayer with 'Our', Jesus reminds us that even in the privacy of our home we remain part of both the family of the Church and the human family. Some Christians would want to add the family of the saints in heaven as well. The important point, however, is that we are not actually alone, even if no one else is physically present. It should encourage us when we find times of prayer difficult. It is not simply up to us. Jesus said the Holy Spirit would help us in our praying, and there are many who have experienced the sense that when their own words fail they are given the words to say, although of course words aren't essential for prayer to be real.

Does prayer feel a solitary activity for you? Is it a struggle or a joy?

Others

It can be helpful as we enter a time of prayer to be quiet, to remember first that we are in God's presence, and then to remember that we are, as it were, surrounded by others. There are those whom we love and who love us. There are friends and colleagues in the fellowship of the faith. There are those among whom we live and work. There are those for whom we have a particular concern at this time – those known to us, and those across the world in need of prayer. While, of course, we have our own needs and reasons for personal gratitude and personal things to confess and be sorry for, it is important that we remember these others – not just in intercession but also in gratitude and in reflection upon the way we are relating to them. Some people find it helpful to keep a prayer list of those they remember in their prayers. For others, a set of photos can be used as a focus for reflecting upon what those people mean to them, holding them in God's presence.

Children are sometimes taught to remember certain people in their prayers – Mum and Dad, siblings, grandparents, friends. The list can become like ticking off a register, names automatically mentioned with a catch-it-all 'God bless them' to round off the prayer. We may smile at that, but we too may find that, almost without thinking about it, we are always praying for the same people. The list never changes. That can be the trouble with lists!

Do you find it helpful to have a list of people you pray for? How do you review the list? How important is it to let people go from the list as well as adding others?

Inclusivity

The most important point about the opening word of Jesus' prayer is that it is addressed to God, 'our' God. 'Our' can be a tricky word. It can be very inclusive so that at its widest we include all people. But it can also be narrowed down in such a way that the 'our' means only those people I like or who are like me. The popular hymn 'Our God reigns' may intend to be inclusive, but it can also be sung to sound both possessive of God and intentionally cutting out of all those who don't see God 'our' way. It can become a tribal chant.

When being most honest, who do you include in the 'our' when you address God as 'our Father'?

As important as our sense of being part of a wider fellowship or humanity is, there are times when we properly come to God as individuals seeking to deepen our relationship with him, bearing our anxieties and joys, our confessions and our thanksgiving, our requests and our adoration. But there is always the danger that what is particular to me overrides my sense of others and that I treat God as my personal possession.

Do you ever reflect on your time of prayer and check how far it has been 'self' concerned and how far it has focused on others?

No man is an island,
entire of itself,
every man is a piece of the continent,
a part of the main.
If a clod be washed away by the sea,
Europe is the less.
As well as if a promontory were.
As well as if a manor of thy friend's
or of thine own were:
any man's death diminishes me,
because I am involved in mankind,
and therefore never send to know for whom the bell tolls;
it tolls for thee.
John Donne

TWO

Heavenly Father

PART A

Experience

Karl was small for his age and not an easy youngster. Usually rather shy and withdrawn, he could on occasions fly into a rage. He had been in care since he was 8, and at 13 he was still having to come to terms with the traumas of the past. He had come home from school one winter afternoon soon after his eighth birthday and found the body of his mother cut up in the bath. His father had done it.

I met Karl in the residential childcare home I visited as part of my pastoral training when I was a theological student. Each Wednesday evening we went to talk and play games with the boys, and on Sundays we held a service for them. One of the staff came up to me after a service and said, 'It's all very good you calling God "Father", but what do you think that says to Karl?' He then told me Karl's story.

I have often pondered on that experience and thought not only about Karl but also about how, for all of us, experience shapes the way we use language. This is especially true of religious language, which by its very nature is so often symbolic and charged with emotion. How far, for example, has my own view of God as Father been shaped by the fact that because of the War I didn't know my father until I was 6? He was the absent presence, distant, someone my mother mentioned from time to time but whom I knew only through photos. Later experience changed all that, but in some ways my father, no matter how loving, was always slightly distant, even to some extent an intruder into the family of my mother and brother and sister.

Jesus and Joseph

We know nothing about Jesus' upbringing apart from the one story when he was 12 when the family, along with the rest of the village, went to Jerusalem for the festival (Luke 2:41-51). His parents acted like any other caring parents: distraught over a missing son. But about his relationship with his parents we can only surmise, though Luke does tell us he was obedient to them. Tradition says that his mother became his first disciple and there is every reason to think that they were very close, although he could also speak quite sharply to her on occasion (John 2:4; see also Matthew 12:46-50).

Of Joseph we know virtually nothing. It has always been assumed that he was rather older than Mary and that he died before Jesus began his public ministry. He has traditionally been thought of as a carpenter (Matthew 13:55; Mark 6:3), but the Greek word used to describe his job could mean someone who worked not only with wood but also with other materials such as metal or stone. It is possible that he was a general builder working either around the village of Nazareth or, perhaps more likely, on the restoration of the nearby town of Sepphoris, which had been destroyed by the Romans in 4 BC. It is reasonable to suppose that Jesus followed his father's trade. The way Jesus used Father as a term for God would indicate that Joseph was a loving father.

Jesus and God

It is almost impossible for us to read passages from the Gospels in which Jesus speaks of God as Father without doing so against the background of the later doctrine of the Trinity. It is understandable if we make the assumption that of course Jesus spoke of God as Father, especially in the intimate way he did, since this is the nature of the Godhead. But that is to read back into the Gospels a later development. How far Jesus was conscious of what might be called his 'divine' nature and the relationship he had within the Godhead is a matter of some speculation that leads us into realms we cannot explore here. Perhaps it is enough to say that in his prayers and in his teaching Jesus showed an intimacy with God whom he called Father to an extent that was remarkable and significant.

There was nothing particularly unusual for Jews to think of God as the Father of the Jewish people (Isaiah 63:16; 64:8; Jeremiah 3:19; 31:9; Malachi 2:10), but not until the Christian era, and then only in late writings, did an individual address God as Father (Sirach 23:1, 4; Wisdom 2:16). Much has been made of the fact that when Jesus did so he used the Aramaic word *Abba*, which was the word most often used by a child and is equivalent to 'Dada' or 'Daddy'. It implies intimacy and trust. This is how Jesus wanted his disciples to understand their relationship with God and the way to address God in prayer. This was new. If Jews wanted to speak to God in prayer, they would have used the form *Abbis*, which was much more formal. Jesus dared to use a term that would normally refer to a human father and applied this to God.

While not absent from the other Gospels, it is in John's Gospel that Jesus is most often reported as speaking of God as 'my Father' and not just 'the Father' or 'your Father'. This builds up a picture of a very close relationship that might imply a kind of equality – although Jesus on one occasion was very clear that the Father was greater than himself (John 14:28). But even if there was not equality, there was an equivalence, as when Jesus says that those who love him will be loved by the Father: 'Whoever does not love me does not keep my words; and the word that you hear is not mine, but is from the Father who sent me' (John 14:24), and whoever hates him hates the Father also (John 15:23). He speaks of being in the Father and of the Father being in him (John 14:11), and says that his words are those of the Father (John 14:24).

Secret code

Although the Gospel writers understood that the relationship between Jesus and his Father was not exactly the same as that between the disciples and the Father, it is clear that they believed Jesus saw it as comparable. As we saw above, the 'our' embraces the disciples in the relationship of Jesus with his Father. In both private prayer and public worship the followers of Jesus were to address God as Father, and the 'Our Father' was seen as a distinctive prayer of the followers of Jesus.

It is possible that, just as making the sign of the fish was a way two people would identify to each other that they were Christians, so also in a time of persecution cryptic codes were used between believers. One of these may well have been the so-called Rotas Square.

ROTAS
OPERA
TENET
AREPO
SATOR

While the use of the Square may have originated in Jewish circles and had other meanings, it has been suggested that it contained a reference to *Pater Noster* (Our Father) when the letters were set out in the form of a cross.

```
                    A
                    P
                    A
                    T
                    E
                    R
          APATERNOSTERO
                    O
                    S
                    T
                    E
                    R
                    O
```

The A at the beginning and O at the end signified Alpha and Omega – the first and last letters of the Greek alphabet and referred to in Revelation: '"I am the Alpha and the Omega", says the Lord God, who is and who was and who is to come, the Almighty' (Revelation 1:8; see also 21:6; 22:13).

Christians have therefore typically and consistently understood God as Father. The use of the Lord's Prayer both encourages and reinforces this relationship. All who are followers of Christ, members of the Body of Christ, the Church, join with each other and with Christ to call God 'Father'. But there are those who would want to go further and say that our relationship with God is grounded in creation and that therefore God is Father of all human beings, whether or not they recognise the fact. Such a view has considerable implications for how Christians view others, not least those of other faiths, but for some this has diluted the evangelistic imperative to preach the good news to all nations and look for 'converts' – those who come to view the fatherhood of God in the way Jesus did.

Father also raises the question, sometimes vexed, of gender. While most people would accept that language about God, even language that Jesus used and taught us to use, is symbolic, there remain those who do not see it entirely that way. In speaking of the mystery that is God at all, we know we are attempting the impossible. Our words are culturally and contextually shaped within a human context. They are the only words we have and are never exhaustive when speaking of God. They are the best we can do, and the alternative is respectful silence. To speak therefore of God as Father is no less symbolic as it is to speak of him as Mother (as Isaiah does – for example, in 66:8). Feminist Christian writers have been vocal in ensuring that our understanding of God is not constrained by language that originates in a male-dominant setting.

The notion of God being a caring, loving Father (or Mother) can feel at odds with the way we often experience the world, not least through history and through the news media, as well as personally. A world that experiences the atrocities of war, the pain of suffering, the distress of victims, may not feel like the creation of a loving Father. We will consider this in more detail when we come to the matter of evil. Here we need to keep in mind that in showing us the Father, Jesus had to undergo his own suffering and painful death. While not exhausting its full meaning, the cross does reveal that God in Jesus knew suffering, and the way Jesus showed compassion to those who suffered around him indicates that God is not careless of our suffering. There is a mystery about suffering, but countless Christians bear witness to the deep sense of being held in the care of a loving Father even while enduring pain and distress. Jesus prayed to his Father in the Garden of Gethsemane that the horrors that he knew lay ahead of him could be taken away, yet in obedience submitted himself to the will of God into whose loving hands he finally commended his spirit as he died on the cross. None of this is a glib answer to those who feel the tension between a world in which there is evil and the relationship they have with a loving God, but it deepens the meaning of what we mean when we speak of God as Father.

Who art in heaven

This phrase immediately plunges us into the question of translation and the version of the Lord's Prayer we use. I was brought up to say, 'Our Father which art in heaven . . .', and did so for decades. The change to 'Our Father who art in heaven . . .' felt to me like a useful piece of updating. But it also signified more than that. It underlined the theological point that when we speak of God we are speaking of a God who, as Jesus has shown us, can only be understood in personal terms. He is not a force or an abstract power. The God who is Father is not simply 'destiny'. He is not a 'thing'. A further updating gave us, 'Our Father in heaven . . .'

In all these versions the implication, if not the emphasis, is upon the location of the Father – 'in heaven'. This is where God has traditionally been understood to reside, and the location of heaven was for centuries obvious – up in the sky beyond the clouds, somewhere beyond the stars, but definitely 'up there'. This, of course, made perfect sense when the common understanding of the cosmos put the earth, initially thought of as flat, at the centre of things, with a region below reserved for all the nasties and a heaven way above us where the gods and the angels reside. Astronomers from the renaissance onwards presented a very different picture, and modern discoveries have shown the complete inadequacy of the earlier picture. Most of what they tell us is complex and almost unimaginable. The numbers alone set the head spinning – the number of galaxies, the number of stars, the size and the distances. Yuri Gagarin, the first man in space, famously announced that he had gone above the clouds but had not found God. It fed the atheistic publicity of Russia at the time.

It is easy both to dismiss the simple cosmology of our ancestors and to scorn the astronaut's assertion, because it actually proved nothing about God. But the reality is that when asked where heaven is, lots of people still point upwards, even though a little vaguely: 'Well, up there, I suppose, somewhere, sort of . . ." Science may have updated our understanding of the cosmos but the symbolism of heaven being 'up' persists. Higher is not only a spatial symbol, it also represents status.

Distant and close

It hasn't only been the scientists who have found the notion of God up in heaven, above the clouds, difficult. In the middle of the twentieth century there was a lot of discussion about the way we speak of where God is and considerable concern about the idea of God being way beyond us, in a distant heaven. It conveyed a sense of a God not only distant in place but also distant in concern. Following the Second World War it was little wonder that people had become disenchanted with a distant, uninvolved God, uncaring about the plight of a world where suffering and evil were all too obvious. Jesus, it was argued, had come from God precisely to demonstrate and to teach us that God is not a distant God but one who is with us, intimate, involved. Far from being 'out there', he is within us, the very ground of our being. The God within, God as Spirit, was increasingly the dominant image of God, and any talk about a God somewhere off in heaven seemed to make him both too detached from our everyday lives and not the kind of Father God Jesus had revealed and taught about. The pendulum had swung from 'out' to 'in' but was in danger of being just as misleading, simply because it was turning a corrective emphasis into an absolute. It was as though God who was 'within' could not also be 'out there'.

Jesus' language about God as Father managed to keep a balance between these two extremes. He gave us a way to understand God that does not have to opt for one image or the other but holds the two together. As we have seen, his typical word for father, even when talking about God, was the intimate, personal word *Abba*. But Jesus also spoke about his 'Father in heaven' and, when talking to his disciples, of 'your Father in heaven'. In doing so he wasn't trying to edge back from the boldness of his radical view of God as *Abba* in order to appease the traditionalists by adding a touch of reverence. He was reflecting a complex understanding of God who, in traditional terms, is both immanent (near) and transcendent (beyond). Reference to heaven does not inevitably imply a 'disinterested distance'. Indeed, Jesus insisted that 'heaven' or 'the kingdom of heaven' is 'at hand'. In Jewish terms this was a reverential way of saying that the rule of God is something close to us, among us. God does not exercise power from a distance but is involved in what goes on in human lives, society and nations.

In speaking of God as 'heavenly' Father, Jesus is not simply saying that God is as loving and caring as the best of earthly fathers/mothers. Rather, he is insisting that God's love and caring are perfect. He is the model of what it is to be loving and caring. Earthly fathers/mothers, at their best, are made in his image. Not the other way round. The qualifying adjective 'heavenly' also means that God is not simply a complacent, indulgent father with whom we are on such close terms that we can wind him around our little finger. The heavenly Father shows what it is to have power and authority while also being loving and caring. They are not alternative ways of being a father/mother. They complement each other. His loving has power (is effective); his caring is authoritative (is not sentimental).

The Gospel accounts convey this through the way they report the compassion Jesus showed in the face of need or distress. We see it when he is approached by lepers or the blind, the guilty or the mad. He cares about their situation and does something about it. Sometimes it is a matter of his responding to the request of others; sometimes, as for example in the account of the woman at Nain, it is Jesus who takes the initiative, moved by the plight of the widow whose only son had died, leaving her not only distraught but very vulnerable (Luke 7:11-17). This account comes in a section of the Gospel where the evangelist has been giving a series of examples of the way in which Jesus' authority is shown through the power of his word. Power and authority come together with love and care. What he does are down-to-earth examples for the way he understands the 'heavenly Father' behaves towards us, the way he is.

This makes it clear that what the prayer is emphasising is not really to do with where God 'lives' but with the very nature of God. To this extent the newer version, which speaks of 'Our heavenly Father', is less misleading than the version which speaks of 'Father in heaven'. Reference to heaven is telling us about the nature and distinctive qualities of this Father rather than providing his address.

PART B
Father

Jack adored his fireman father. He was Jack's hero, his very best friend. He'd always been there to look after Jack, to have fun with, to give advice, to discuss things. Jack looked upon his childhood as a very happy time, and even as a teenager things had been pretty good. As a grown-up it was always to his father that Jack would go for advice. In his prayers he found it absolutely natural to pray to God as Father.

Lorraine was an only child and her father had never wanted her, and he made it plain. He had wanted a boy, and he either belittled her or tried to get her to be as much like as a boy as possible. She hated rock climbing and was scared of canoeing but he made her do them. She even began to hate herself, and before he walked out on the family she had begun harming herself. She never found it easy to pray to God as Father. She would always pray to Jesus whom she saw as the wonderful older brother she had never had.

These may be extremes, but our experience of our parents does have an effect on the way we pray. At one end of the scale our parents can be the most important model for our lives. At the other end, our lives may be lived in reaction to all that we felt was damaging about their relationship with us. For most of us there's a mixture of both. If we are people who pray, this is certain to have some impact.

The majority of us take the way we pray most naturally as just the way it is and seldom think too much about it. But it is worth reflecting on what we do. In my experience most people do most naturally, but not necessarily exclusively, pray either to God or to Jesus.

Take time to consider your own prayer pattern. Is there a discernible preference? Do you have any idea why this should be so? Do you think it matters?

Loving

When Jesus taught us to call God 'Father', he was not only telling us how to address God but also encouraging us to see God in a certain way. For Jesus, God was loving, caring, forgiving. He wanted us to see God in this way as well. For some of us this builds on what we have always experienced of our own parents. For others, the loving Father God Jesus taught about provides a powerful compensation for the loving parents they never knew.

What feelings are uppermost when you think about God and pray to him – love? fear? awe? hope? closeness? distance? Or does it just depend on what is going on in your life at any particular time?

Initiative

Our feelings may well change and sometimes we may feel very hesitant, even ashamed, about approaching God in prayer at all. Jesus told us that God the loving Father doesn't just wait for us to be good or to be in a religious frame of mind, longing to talk to him, to be in his presence. Those things may happen, but the Father, Jesus said, comes out to meet us no matter what, and that includes when we are at our worst. Think of these three of Jesus' parables: the lost sheep, the lost coin, the prodigal son (Luke 15:3-32).

As we think about our own relationship with God as Father we might well reflect on those who have lost or are separated from their parents, especially when that is at a young age. We may personally know children who have been abused or abandoned. But even if we do not, there is sadly no shortage of stories and pictures of children cut off from their loved ones through war or violence, accident or neglect. We can take them to the loving Father in our prayers – sometimes that is all we can do.

In thinking of God as loving Mother/Father we may wish to reflect not only on our relationship with our parents but also, if we have them, our relationship with our children. If our own image of God has, in part at least, been shaped by our relationship with our parents, it follows that how we relate to our children will have its effect upon the way they view God. That can be quite a sobering and challenging thought.

How far do you feel your relationship with your children has helped them to view God as a loving Father?

Heavenly

Ultimately, of course, there is a difference between even the most loving parent and our Father God. Jesus pointed to this distinction by speaking of our 'heavenly' Father.

What do you feel are the most significant differences between God as heavenly Father and what you see as even the best earthly parents?

In part, your answer to such a question may well reflect what you think about heaven itself. For some, talk of heaven is too remote and speculative to be of much value. They find any of the pictures thinkers and poets and artists have come up with less than helpful. Others, of course, have very clear ideas built on biblical and other images. For most of us, talk of heaven will at some point or other raise the thought of death, our own and that of others, not least of our parents.

Do you think we should pray for those who have died? How do you pray for those who are dying and for those who are grieving?

We know that if the earthly tent we live in is destroyed, we have a building from God, a house not made with hands, eternal in the heavens.   *2 Corinthians 5:1*

THREE

Hallowed Be Thy Name

PART A

God comes first

The commonest idea about prayer is that it is a request, a wish, a plea. It seeks to obtain something or for something to happen. It's asking God to do something, to provide something, to enable something, to prevent something. And most often that something revolves around me – my wants, my needs, my life, my fears. Put as baldly as that makes it sound as though people are pretty selfish when it comes to praying. And when pushed, that's probably what we are. Even our thanks are most likely to be thanks for something that we have had, something we've achieved, something that has had an impact on our lives. It would be an exaggeration, of course, to say that all our prayer is like this – but it's the way it is a good bit of the time.

In offering his disciples a pattern of how they should pray, Jesus was aware of this self-centred tendency, and this next phrase of his prayer acts as a kind of brake upon our self-concern. It reminds us that before we start asking we should acknowledge the one we are addressing, and do so in a way that places the emphasis on him. When it comes to prayer, 'God first' is the order Jesus taught us.

Hallowed

The first petition, this first request of the Lord's Prayer, focuses our attention on God, not on ourselves, not even on other people. We ask for God's name to be 'hallowed'. That isn't a word that is greatly used these days. Unexpectedly, it does crop up occasionally in the context of sport. Fans or commentators can talk about 'hallowed turf' – for football it could be Wembley, for rugby it would be Twickenham and for tennis it is Wimbledon. These grounds have a special significance and importance. To play at one of these venues is to play on 'hallowed' turf. Hallowed in this context implies a special kind of respect, or reverence even, with all the associations of the pinnacle of the sport.

The more usual context is that of churchyards and cemeteries – the 'hallowed ground' of burial. It is ground that has been consecrated or blessed and has therefore become sacred, with all the associations of reverence and mystery that surround the dead. It's a place of memories, where sensibilities are not to be taken lightly but treated with respect. In fact, of course, this doesn't only have to refer to graveyards. Any ground that has been blessed may be considered 'hallowed' – be that blessing by a Christian priest or by a dignitary of another religion. Churches and temples, mosques and gurdwaras all rest on hallowed ground, and those who enter are called to pay appropriate respect. To a Native American all ground is hallowed, in much the same way as all life is sacred to a Buddhist.

'Revered' and 'respected' are possible synonyms and are more readily understood, but they lack the depth of meaning that 'hallowed' holds. Sacred and holy add depth, especially when one realises that 'holy' is not just a pious way of saying 'good'. Holy conveys the idea of being set aside for a sacred purpose, of being morally and religiously distinctive, not of the common run of things. But perhaps the very strangeness of the word 'hallowed' and the effort we have to make to reach its meaning is a good reason to retain it as part of this prayer. Without resonances and subtlety which go beyond easy access, our language lacks richness and depth.

Name

Jesus has taught us then to ask for God's name to be hallowed. But why this emphasis upon God's name? In our common usage, to name something is to give it a label; it is a way of distinguishing it from something else – a spade rather than a shovel, a rose rather than a marigold, a bus rather than a car. The more specific the name, the more we can pin down exactly what is being referred to – a Rolls Royce rather than a Ford, a 2003 Ghost rather than a 2010 Phantom.

Names identify, but they do more than that. We only have to think about what goes into the parents' choice in giving a name to their baby. All kinds of associations of family and place, of admiration and celebrity, can be present. It is often more by luck than judgement that a name given at birth conveys what a child will actually grow into. The mother of a friend of mine was called Primrose. She was a large, rosy-cheeked farmer's wife with a voice that could travel across a hundred-acre field. Her father-in-law was once heard to remark, 'Primrose? More like a ruddy peony!'

To a Hebrew, a name was even more significant. It was the reality it conveyed. If you knew a person's name you knew the person; it was the person. We only have to think of significant times in Bible accounts when a person's name was changed – not because they had got fed up with what they had been called and wanted a change, but because they themselves or their status had significantly changed. God changed Abram's name to Abraham. Abram probably means 'exalted father', but following the covenant God made with him, that name became Abraham, meaning 'father of a multitude of nations' (Genesis 17:1-5). Jesus changed Symeon's (Simon's) name to Peter, which in Aramaic was *Cephas*, and in Greek *Petros*, meaning 'rock'. In John's Gospel this was how Jesus first referred to Simon, a stalwart, reliable person. Matthew records Jesus as giving Simon the name Peter and explaining the change in terms of Peter being the 'rock,' the solid foundation upon which the church was to be built. (Matthew 16:13-18). This was more than just a nickname, like the boxer Rocco Marciano who was known as Rocky. It was to convey Peter's character and role.

Interestingly, one of the most famous name changes, Saul to Paul, is not strictly a name change at all. Saul was his Jewish name, Paul his name in Latin, and as both a Jew and a Roman citizen he had these dual names. In the context of his upbringing and his association with the Pharisees it would have been normal for him to use his Hebrew name. But after his conversion he saw his mission as spreading out into the Roman Empire, where use of the name Paul was much more appropriate. In this instance it speaks more of his understanding of his work and circumstances than of someone else giving him a change of name.

In the story of creation in Genesis 2, God formed all the creatures and then he brought them to Adam to give them their names, 'and whatever the man called each living creature, that was its name' (Genesis 2:19). This illustrates what is made explicit in the account in chapter 1 where we are told that God gave to man and woman 'dominion over the fish of the sea and over the birds of the air and over every living thing that moves upon the earth' (Genesis 1:28). To name something or to know the name of something was understood to give you power over it.

After Jacob had wrestled all night with the strange figure (Genesis 32:22-32), he demanded a blessing before he would let him go. Jacob was asked what his name was, and the stranger changed it from Jacob to Israel because he had 'striven with God and with humans, and [had] prevailed' (Genesis 32:28). But when Jacob asked the stranger for his name, no name was given. At the burning bush, Moses too asked God his name, but all he was given was the enigmatic reply, 'I am who I am' (Exodus 3:13, 14). To know the name meant Moses would know the person, the one with the power to effect the freedom from Egypt that the Israelites longed for.

This specific relationship between the name and the reality meant that when it came to God's name the Hebrews treated it with such respect (they hallowed it) that they normally found other ways to refer to God or declined from giving the name in full. The second of the Ten Commandments made it clear that God's name was not to be misused or taken in vain (Exodus 20:7). This wasn't simply a ban on bad language but on the use of the power of God's name incorrectly, such as in spells. The deepest misuse of God's name was not through the spoken word but through action. The way we behave shows how we 'hallow' God's name, his reality in our lives.

The Lord's Prayer asks not simply that we show respect for God's name but also that God will hallow it. It is a request that God will be the God Jesus is revealing to us, and that he will do so by his actions. Nowhere is this made more obvious than in the cross, in which the name of God was 'glorified', shown in action, 'hallowed'. Here in the death of Christ God, who is love, was demonstrating the love and transforming forgiveness which is the core of his nature. Self-giving love is God's reality, his name.

PART B

In a BBC lecture a few years ago, Daniel Barenboim spoke of the importance of the silence out of which music emerges, that point at the start of a performance as the conductor waits for just the right moment, the right silence, before the first note sounds. We might say something similar about prayer – that it arises not from our words but from the silence. In that silence we have the opportunity to enter the presence of God, to reflect on the nature of the one we are about to speak and listen to.

As important as words are, they are always ultimately inadequate. It is one of the reasons why such a religion as Zoastrianism has more than one hundred names for God. Each one catches only a part of what God is and means, and even all together they cannot express the fullness of God. The words with which we clothe God are all second-hand, none his own, none exactly capturing who he is.

Do you have a favourite name or title for God?

Silence

How might we use that silence out of which the words of our prayers emerge? We can use it to quieten our hearts and minds, to turn aside from all the noisy bustle of our lives. A time to focus on God. Some people find it helpful to have an object – a candle or flower or picture perhaps – upon which to concentrate in a relaxed way as they move in heart and spirit into the presence of God.

How helpful do you find it to begin prayer with silence? Do you have a particular way to help you focus your thoughts on God?

It is also good to be aware of the nature of the God who is with us in that silence. Jesus' prayer tells us we can approach God as a loving Father, someone who will welcome us, who will not dismiss us as unworthy, not be too busy to listen. But he is the 'heavenly' Father who is the creator God, the Lord of all. So in focusing upon him we do well to come in an attitude of awe and adoration. We are not required to cower before God, but we are called to respect who God is. There is a proper reverence to be shown. That can make it sound all rather stuffy or pompous, but not if such reverence arises from a deepening sense of gratitude for all that God is and does.

As you begin to pray, it might be helpful to think about what in particular it is that God has done or is doing in your life and the lives of others for which you are especially grateful. Such gratitude for what God does can lead to adoration for what God is.

God's name

In the earlier part of this chapter we noted that in the Hebrew way of thinking, a name not only provides a way of identifying a person or an object but also encapsulates their identity. Jesus' prayer calls upon God to 'hallow' his name, to be true to his very being. This implies that we also should honour God's name. More than that, it reflects the way in which God respects our name, our identity. We would hardly expect anything less from a loving heavenly Father. But in honouring us, God calls us to honour and to respect ourselves. There is a proper self-confidence he wants us all to have.

How well do you love yourself? Are you able to draw upon the fact that God 'honours' you to find the self-confidence he wants you to have?

Personal worth

I think that one of the primary purposes of education is to help every child grow into a proper sense of their personal worth. Low self-esteem is so common and so damaging. In our relationships and through our prayers we should seek to help others to grow in a sense of their own worth. It is important that at least some of our prayers should be for people by name, and that as we name them before God we not only think of their needs but also give thanks for what they are and what they do.

> Do you give thanks to God for other people – not only for what they do but also for what they are? Do your prayers of thanks lead to expressing those thanks to the people themselves? It could do wonders for their self-esteem. Just think what being thanked does for yours.

A newspaper item quoted in the BBC programme *The News Quiz*:

> The Low Esteem Group will meet in the village hall on Wednesday. Please use the back door.

FOUR

Thy Kingdom Come

PART A

Nationalism

I am writing this in the week that followed the United Kingdom's decision to leave the European Union. The arguments for Brexit, as for Remain, were varied, but among them was the desire for 'independence', for a recovery of Britain's sovereignty. People no longer wanted to be ruled from Brussels. They wanted their country back. It was a popular and seemingly straightforward message, appealing to patriotism. It reflected what many older voters saw as 'being a great nation' again. In the months and years ahead we will see if their hopes are going to be realised.

There is nothing unique about such sentiments. Nationalism has been a feature of politics across the centuries. In the nineteenth century it was nationalism that drove the fight against autocracy in Europe. It was nationalist movements that led the fight for freedom from the power and rule of the British Empire. The break-up of the Soviet Union came about in part through the demands of peoples insisting on their independence, their national rights. In the immediate aftermath of the referendum outcome in Britain, right-wing nationalist parties in a number of European countries called for their own referenda. Nationalism is a powerful motivator for change.

In the time of Jesus there was a strong nationalist movement in Israel that was looking to escape the domination of Rome. Israel longed to be an independent people, ruled not by a foreign power but by their God. As so often happens, the way to achieve independence was understood very differently. In broad terms, there were two main approaches.

Bringing in the kingdom

Firstly, there was the 'stand up and fight' party. The leaders were the Zealots who believed that the only way to achieve freedom was to take up arms. Some may have done so reluctantly, others may have gloried in the sense of a righteous battle, but the Zealots were the 'guerrillas', the independence fighters of their day. They believed that the longed-for time when God would rule again could only be accomplished by heroic acts of violence. There had been a number of armed rebellions, not least the one in Galilee when Jesus was growing up. Far from achieving freedom, it had been put down by the Romans with cruel ferocity. But it did not end the Zealot party, nor their cause. Rome's actions reinforced a sense of injustice, of the need to fight against the evil of foreign domination. Jesus himself may have been attracted by the Zealot cause and approach. This is certainly one way of understanding the struggle he experienced in the third of the temptations he wrestled with in the wilderness (Matthew 4:8-10). There he came to reject the ways of violent power as being the approach of the same evil powers that already dominated the world. If God's kingdom was to come, it was not by following the path of what he saw as evil power but rather by commitment to the ways of God, which he had come to understand as being radically different. Even so, one of his disciples – Simon – was, or had been, a member of the Zealot party.

The second approach to the question of how God's kingdom was to be established came from the Pharisees. It is only fair to acknowledge that in the Gospels, the Pharisees get a poor press. Modern scholarship has tended to come to the view that Jesus had much more in common with them than is indicated by the accounts in the Gospels. Be that as it may, it is equally clear that Jesus did not wholeheartedly embrace their approach. The Pharisees believed that the way forward was not by force of arms but by the power of righteous living. They were sticklers for the rules, for what they believed were God's injunctions for the moral and holy life – both individually and for the whole people. They believed that when the people once more became a holy people, following God's law, then God would act and bring in his kingdom. The nation would be freed from its oppressors and from the desecration of their land. As Jesus was quick to point out, the danger of this approach was that it led to a sanctimonious hypocrisy. It shackled people into the observation of myriads of rules that did not bring a fullness of living but an exaggerated legalism.

Undoubtedly there were other less extreme approaches. Many ordinary people would have been longing for God to act without them having to take up arms or follow a narrow moralism. There were those who faithfully looked to God, lived in hope and prayed for the day of God's intervention to come. Simon and Anna may have been just such people (Luke 2:25-38). There were also those who, like the Sadducees, had no expectations at all, even though the situation was desperate.

The coming of the kingdom

For those who did expect God to act, the language of those expectations can be summarised as 'a looking forward to the coming of God's kingdom'. In its narrowest terms, this meant national independence in an Israel that was free from foreign rule. Its emphasis would be upon geographical locality. But Hebrew thought, less than our own, saw God's kingdom not so much in terms of the national boundaries of God's control than in the rule of God in the hearts and minds of the people. And this required not simply people coming round to God's way of thinking, as it were, but for God himself to make a decisive move. His kingdom coming was an expression of God's coming among and on behalf of his people in power and as King. This supernatural action was seen by some in highly dramatic and apocalyptic terms, and this would have been fed by such literature in the Hebrew Scriptures as the book of Daniel.

What the Gospels tell us is that the kingdom had come. What everyone had been looking for had in fact happened. According to Mark, Jesus' preaching could be summarised as 'The time is fulfilled, and the kingdom of God has come near' (Mark 1:15; see also Matthew 4:17).

For Luke too, the heart of the Good News that Jesus preached was 'the kingdom of God' (Luke 4:43). When Jesus sent out his disciples, he told them that the news they should proclaim was, 'The kingdom of heaven has come near [or, is at hand]' (Matthew 10:7). There had been no successful rebellion against Rome. The whole population had not followed the teaching of the Pharisees. There had been no thunderous rending of the skies. So what had happened? Simply, Jesus had come. This was, according to the Gospels, the turning point, the radical moment, the divine action. With the coming of Jesus, the kingdom, the rule of God, had come.

Here or still to come

And yet, here in the prayer Jesus taught his followers, is the request that it will come. We might be forgiven if we ask, 'Well, has the kingdom come or not?' It feels less than clear to say, 'It has come, and is still to come.' We might understand it this way. God's rule, his kingdom, is to be seen in total obedience and commitment to God's way. Christians believe this is what Jesus uniquely lived out, and in him God's kingdom did come. But we do not see this in all lives. The rule of God is still something to be realised, and so we are taught to pray for its coming. If we ask what such lives would look like, then we need to look at Jesus' life and listen to what he taught about the kingdom. And there was plenty of such teaching – just think of all the parables that mention the kingdom of God or the kingdom of heaven, which was just a way of saying the same thing without using the name of God.

One of the great debates about the person of Jesus concerns the way we understand his divinity and his humanity. Differences on this led to divisions in the Church, the declaration of heresy, even violent conflict. Orthodoxy became convinced that, while not easy, Christians have to hold the two together: Jesus is both divine and human. The implication for our present discussion is that when we say Jesus was totally obedient and committed to God's will, we are not saying he was simply a very good person. We are saying that God was showing what God's rule looks like in a human life.

The kingdom is not something we can conjure up – not by a fighting zeal, not by moral rectitude. The rule of God is, in fact, an act of God. It is his gift made present among us. But, like all gifts, the gift has to be received, appropriated. It does need a human response. It does need struggling for, it does need lives of holy integrity. The individual heart responding to God's gift of his rule (his grace) does matter. But it means also more than this. For the way Jesus lived out God's rule shows that it is not just a matter of individual piety. His concern for the poor and the marginalised, for the sick and the outcast, for social justice and for a welcome to all, revealed a kingdom that was not simply for the Jews, and is certainly not restricted to Christians. It is for all. It is not a private matter of faith and religious practice, but is concerned about society and the arena of all human living.

The kingdom as gift

This is primarily God's work. It is not simply a matter of human effort and progress, as some have argued in the past. We have learnt all too tragically that the advance of goodness is not guaranteed. We may have made advances in human freedom in some areas, but there is no steady and inevitable progress. Our ways of creating horror as well as freedom have simply increased with our technological advances. As Jesus taught us, we need to continue to pray, and work, for God's kingdom to come and to be realised among us. In Christ it has come; in us it still needs to come. To put it in terms related to my opening comments in this section, the referendum vote made its decision on 23 June 2016, but its outcomes will take years to be realised. The decisive moment is only a beginning. We live in that continuing time between the kingdom having come and still to be realised.

When we pray for the coming of the kingdom, we need to come to terms with just what a serious and demanding request that is. It makes demands on we who pray for God's rule. Its implications are there in the story of Jesus – in his dealings with others and in his obedience to the Father. And there is glory in that. But it is also to be seen in the cross. To live the life of God's rule makes demands – upon God and also upon us.

PART B

When I was applying to go to university it was a requirement to have an O level pass in Latin to get into some of the older universities. Whatever the educational value of studying Latin might have been, there were lots of us who wondered why on earth we had to study a 'dead' language. No one spoke it. Unlike 'living' languages, it was not evolving or developing. By contrast, English is always developing. Every year, the Oxford English Dictionary has to be updated to include new words that have entered common usage.

Anticipointment

A word that has recently been coined, which may or may not catch on enough to get into the dictionary, is 'anticipointment'. It's been defined as:

> The state of mind resulting from excitedly anticipating a strongly promoted product, event, film, etc, and then being disappointed when it fails to meet the expectations generated by this promotion.
>
> *Wiktionary*

In the early Church there must have been a great deal of excited anticipation surrounding the coming of God's kingdom. Jesus had said so much about it. He had told his disciples to pray for it. Many believed that Jesus' death and resurrection had inaugurated the coming of the kingdom. And that was true in many ways – but not with the dramatic arrival of God's new era in the way they had been hoping for. No doubt there were those who suffered anticipointment.

Our perspective on this has inevitably changed somewhat with the passing of the centuries, but it raises an important spiritual point: how do we deal with disappointment in our prayer life while still retaining a genuine sense of hope?

The coming of the kingdom

It would be easy to just give up on the hope as though it doesn't really matter. It would be easy to become cynical about God ever doing anything about it. It would be easy to just drop the whole idea. But there in Jesus' prayer is the regular reminder that the kingdom mattered to him, and he felt it mattered for those who follow him. So he told them to pray for its coming.

> What does the coming of God's kingdom mean to you? Does it ever enter your prayers apart from in the Lord's Prayer? Do you long for God's rule to take over?

When you consider the state of our world today, the number of disputes and wars, the corruption and fraud in governments and big business, we might well long for God to take over, and get impatient that he doesn't. Impatience can lead to disillusionment and to questioning whether God cares, or even if there is a God at all.

> Are you ever disappointed with God? Does delay feel like he is not interested, doesn't care? How easy do you find it to be patient – to wait on God's timing?

Partnership

The coming of the kingdom is neither simply up to God nor entirely up to us. There is a partnership. We can do something to help bring in the kingdom even though it will never be just up to us. We can reflect on the values of the kingdom – on justice, generosity, love, openness and forgiveness, and see how we act out these values. Prayer isn't just a matter of asking that God should make people more just, more forgiving, more loving. We need to ask ourselves what *we* can do to be more just, more forgiving, more loving.

It can be helpful to keep a list of the people we pray for. But it might be just as helpful to keep a list of things we can do which relate to our prayers.

What might you do to put kingdom values into practice and help bring the kingdom nearer? You cannot do everything, but a few very specific actions should be possible – with God's help.

Patience with others is Love, Patience with self is Hope, Patience with God is Faith.
Adel Bestavros[3]

---

3. www.quotes.net.

FIVE

Thy Will Be Done

PART A

This is the third of the requests that come at the beginning of the Lord's Prayer, and all three focus on God, not on ourselves. Given the very brief and succinct way in which Jesus taught his disciples to pray, we might feel that this is a bit excessive. But it emphasises the fact that in prayer it is important to put God first – the honouring (hallowing) of his name (his very nature), the activating of his rule (his kingdom), and here the primacy of his will. We are invited in these phrases to call upon God to be true to his holy character, to make real the gift of his sovereignty in the world and in our lives, and to do what he wills. The three all hang together. They all say, in effect, may God be the kind of God Jesus spoke of as Father and may that be seen in his actions.

But the focus on God does not leave us out of the picture. It is not only that God is asked to be true to himself. In making that request we are pledging ourselves to honour who he is and to see that we live as those acknowledging the kingship, the rule of this Father God. Our prayers not only reveal the kind of God we believe in, but they also have implications for the way we should behave. That is now made explicit in terms of God's will. What we believe to be God's will tells us what kind of God we discover him to be. It also carries with it the challenge for us who make the prayer that we live according to that will.

God's action

At one level it all looks very simple. May what God wants, happen. In practice, however, this is quite a complex issue. A few questions might help us to break it down:

1. Does everything that happens happen because God wills it?

2. How do we discover God's will?

3. What prevents us from doing what God wants?

4. How can we live more in accordance with God's will?

For centuries it has been accepted that God can do everything. He is omnipotent, all-powerful. He would not be God if he weren't. But it has also been recognised that things happen that he does not want to happen. This isn't because he couldn't prevent them if he wanted to, but rather that if he is to be the kind of God he is, he has to allow them to happen. In a dictator that would look like weakness. In a loving God who is our Father it is a strength. Love cannot do everything. It cannot be unloving. So God cannot want to do or actually do what would be unloving towards his creation. However mysterious it may be, however much we find it difficult to understand, the fact is that whatever God does, whatever he wills, has to be loving, with a love that is in accordance with his living nature.

If everything is going smoothly for us that seems to be fine. We are happy, we are well, we are secure, we have a loving family and friends, life is good. God has been good to us, he has been loving. But what if life is tough, we are not well, we are vulnerable, we are lonely, bad things have happened to us or to those we love? It is not so easy then to believe there is a loving God. Even if we don't believe he actually wanted there to be bad things, how can he be loving if he doesn't prevent such things? And if he can't prevent them, how can he be all-powerful? It doesn't feel as if the circle can be squared. Either he can do everything but isn't loving, or he is loving and can't be all-powerful. Tussling with the problem and with the bad situation they are experiencing leads some people to conclude that God doesn't exist at all. Certainly not the Father God Jesus talked about.

We live in an age when people are much more ready to question and blame those in authority for what goes wrong in their lives than would have been the case in earlier days. We are certainly more vociferous and less resigned. Past generations were more prepared, for example, to see their troubles as part of God's will. It may have been said with a shrug of resignation or as a simple statement of faith but words such as, 'We'll have to make the best of it. It's God's will,' were commonplace. This attitude prevailed because some disasters were mysterious – disease was less understood, natural disasters were readily accepted as 'acts of God'. They didn't conclude that God was either a tyrant or that he didn't exist at all. But as scientific and medical knowledge developed and the processes behind illness and dramatic events in nature were better understood, this began to change. There was a greater scepticism and people were more prepared to be very open about their doubts.

Fatalism

A simplistic belief that everything that happens is God's will can lead to a fatalism that inhibits human action and the drive for knowledge and progress. If a person is ill and it is believed that the illness was sent by God and he wants this person to be ill, then to try to prevent it would be an act against God. Medical research would be sinful. And there have certainly been some who have taken such an extreme view. If an earthquake is an act of God, then, according to this way of thinking, there is nothing that can or should be done about it other than submit to God's will. Stronger houses would not have been designed. Care in planning where houses are built would not have been considered. To that extent it is a good thing that these extreme views have not won the day.

Jesus clearly showed us that this form of determinism is not the way to understand God's will. He was never resigned in his attitude towards sickness and disease. Indeed, he saw it as a focal point in his struggle against what was opposed to God's will. His healings were a sign of the victory of a loving God over the forces of Satan. Jesus was not a fatalist. In his parable about where to build a house, he didn't suggest that it should be built on sand and its well-being left to God. He gave a full place for human action and responsibility. In his struggle in the Garden of Gethsemane he was not hitting out against a predetermined force he could not change. He was facing the desperate implications of what it was to be obedient to the Father whose love for the world meant that he would have to suffer – not only Jesus but God too. There is a cost to love, and in obedience to love there is sometimes a heavy cost.

Why?

That does not, of course, answer all the questions we can have about why people get sick, why there are disasters that wreck lives. There is not a slick or quick answer to the questions about why this world is one in which such disasters can happen, where children die of cancer or why elderly suffer from dementia. Our knowledge may gradually unravel the 'how' of such things, but for the person who believes in God it can still leave the 'why'. For some, the questions break their faith. For others, there is a kind of resignation that admits it has no answers but holds on to a belief in God and his goodness, hard as that sometimes is. There is a trust that believes that God is loving and that the way the world is, with all its problems of illness and disaster, is the only world a loving God could produce which allows both a freedom within creation and a freedom for human beings to make a choice to follow such a God or not, to grow in faith or to reject faith. It is a world in which the possibilities of love offered and freely responded to are present, but it is also a world where the possibility that such love will be rejected also exists. It is the arena for the possibility of freely choosing to grow into the humanity God longs for. In the midst of a tragic heartbreak such a faith can be difficult to hang on to, and for some all they can say is, 'It hurts. I don't understand and I just don't know what to believe.' They cling on by the skin of their teeth, praying that the pain will ease and that they will be held by God in the darkness. To do anything more is impossible. To do anything less would be to give up on God completely.

Such struggles, emotional, spiritual and intellectual, together with the greater knowledge we have about the way the world works, means that it can feel too simplistic just to say 'it's God's will' and leave it at that. But as we saw just now, Jesus shows us that belief in and obedience to the Father's will is not fatalistic resignation. But nor is the questioning of God's will rebellion. It is all part of a relationship in which hard things happen, where everything is not rosy. There remains mystery that we may not be able to resolve but which we can enter into and grow through. And for Jesus and for us, it is the mystery of the will of a loving Father.

How?

This raises the question, however, about just how God does act in the world. Indeed, does he act at all, and if so, in what ways? There are two extreme possibilities:

A. that God constantly acts, micro-managing his world so that in his love he manipulates the weather, he stops runaway cars, he fixes job applications. So people pray for a parking space and believe God made it possible for them to find one. Students do no work and believe God will make it possible for them to pass their exams with flying colours. God is the fixer, tinkering with his world to make it right – for me.

B. that God has set the universe going and is now on his holidays, leaving it, and us, to get along as best we can. He does nothing because he wants his universe to be free. He wants human beings to learn to take responsibility for their actions without expecting him to constantly get them out of a mess. The only prayer is, 'Help us to make wise decisions,' and even that help could feel like interference.

Even when put in that rather crude way, it is possible to see that each position has an element of truth about it. God does act, and people's prayers do get answered, but he also looks to us to grow in being responsible for what we do. That means having to face the consequences of our actions without God constantly stepping in to sort them out.

Some modern theologians have sought to understand God's activity without going to either extreme by seeing God as much more part of the whole process of the way we and the world works. So he is not 'out there', poking his finger in when required, nor is he simply sitting on his hands. Rather, he is intimately involved in all that there is from the inside, as it were, while respecting the nature of matter he has created/is creating. He does not manipulate the jet stream to make the sun shine on the parish garden party. He does not mend the hole in the ozone layer our technology has created. He does not prevent the terrorist from pulling the trigger. But he is active: inviting, guiding, enabling those responses in nature and in us that follow the flow of his loving intention. Prayer becomes less a matter of trying to persuade God to do things we want than seeking to align ourselves with what God wants. As Jesus prayed, 'Not what I want but what you want' (Matthew 26:39). Because he respects the nature he has created, it means that those processes which make it possible for our world to develop and be sustained are also processes that in other situations can cause problems. So volcanic eruptions help to replenish the mineral resources of the earth but can also devastate areas of population. Cell mutation has made evolution possible but can also produce cancers.

Would it be possible for God to have created a world in which only the good things happen? Who can tell? All we know is that this is the world he did create, and if we follow Jesus' example and teaching, he did so as a loving Father, not as a fickle despot. Our own freedom of choice can make for some terrible situations of oppression and of injustice, but that same freedom is equally the basis for some wonderful things to happen and for the way we grow in responsibility. It remains a mystery, but love holds such glorious possibilities. For love to express itself in this way, God took the risk of making his world the way it is. If those theologians are right in saying God is involved in the very processes of his universe, then he shares in its horrors as well as in its marvels.

There will no doubt still be times when we feel God has failed to act when we would have wanted him to – not necessarily for our sake but for the sake of others. For one family, their prayer seems to have been answered and a person has grown better when medical opinion said there was no hope. For another, prayer just as fervent was offered and there was no cure. We do not understand. But it is how we respond to whatever we face that makes the difference. To do so with trust and faith is always easier said than done.

God's will

If we are to act in accordance with God's will, then it is obvious that we need to have a reasonably clear idea what God's will is. In a general sense we could say that all that God wills is loving. Since God is love (1 John 4:8), he cannot will that which is not loving, and so long as we do what is loving we will know we are doing what he wants. But love is a tricky word, partly because it is used in so many different situations and with so many different nuances. It includes our likes, our emotions, our aesthetic sense, our wills, our relationships, our tastes.

For the Christian, the only way we can be sure we have a reasonably clear idea what we mean when talking about a loving God is to look at what the life and teachings of Jesus show us. Without being exhaustive, the following list will give us some idea:

- It is universal; it's for all: 'For God so loved the world . . .' (John 3:16).

- It enters the situation of the loved: 'The Word became flesh and lived among us' (John 1:14).

- It is humble: he 'did not regard equality with God as something to be exploited, but emptied himself, taking the form of a slave, being born in human likeness' (Philippians 2:6, 7).

- It is compassionate: 'When Jesus saw her weeping, and the Jews who came with her also weeping, he was greatly disturbed in spirit and deeply moved. He said, "Where have you laid him?" They said to him, "Lord, come and see." Jesus began to weep' (John 11:33-5).

- It is costly and not just for those we like: 'God proves his love for us in that while we still were sinners Christ died for us' (Romans 5:8).

- It is ultimately victorious: 'For I am convinced that neither death, nor life, nor angels, nor rulers, nor things present, nor things to come, nor powers, nor height, nor depth, nor anything else in all creation, will be able to separate us from the love of God in Christ Jesus our Lord' (Romans 8:38,39).

In his famous 'hymn to love', Paul lists what he considers true love to be like. It is thought that he based his list on what he believed to be true of Jesus. It has been described as a portrait of Jesus (1 Corinthians 13:4-8, 13):

Love is patient; love is kind; love is not envious or boastful or arrogant or rude. It does not insist on its own way; it is not irritable or resentful; it does not rejoice in wrongdoing, but rejoices in the truth. It bears all things, believes all things, hopes all things, endures all things.

Love never ends. But as for prophecies, they will come to an end . . . And now faith, hope, and love abide, these three; and the greatest of these is love.

In summary, we might say that the love we see in Jesus, and therefore the love of God, is a self-giving, compassionate, forgiving, accepting and challenging regard for all. What God wills springs from this kind of love, and if we want to do what God wants, then our choices, our words, our actions need to spring from a love like this.

When it comes to particular choices and actions, they will not only be informed by this overall picture of the nature of love, but also by what we read in the Bible, what we see in the example of others, what we discover through our prayer and our relationship with God, what we decide through careful thought. We will not always get it clear; we will not always get it right. We will not always feel that our choices are entirely in our hands. Even when we do feel we know what God wants of us, it is not always easy to do it. We will fail. We will sin. Even St Paul found that (Romans 7:21). Knowing and doing God's will is not simple. It is part of our lifetime's spiritual journey. In his love he gives us his Spirit to guide us and help us, and his forgiveness to pick us up when we do fail.

Our failure

If God's will is loving and loving is good, why do we fail to carry out God's will? Simply to say it is because we are sinners may be true, but that doesn't get us very far. Motives are complex and various. As we saw above in the case of Paul, we don't always even understand ourselves. Something gets hold of us and we do things we know we shouldn't. Some people explain that in terms of spiritual forces, personalised as Satan or the devil. Others see it more in terms of inner drives built into us through the process of evolution.

Again a simple list, while not being exhaustive, may help:

- We simply don't know what God's will is – either because we just cannot fathom it out or because we haven't tried to find out, or a bit of each.

- We feel it demands more of us than we can face.

- We are afraid of the consequences – embarrassment, scorn, being thought of badly, punishment.

- We just want to do things our way – it feels easier, better, more fun.

- The pressure of others on us.

So often it is fear that is at the root of not doing what is right: fear of consequences, fear of others, fear of missing out, fear of being rejected.

It is no coincidence that the most frequently occurring phrase in the Bible is, 'Fear not'. And it is no surprise that it is perfect love that casts out fear (1 John 4:18). Sometimes it is God, sometimes it is other people, sometimes it is ourselves we fail to love. Jesus urged us, 'commanded' us, to love – God, others and ourselves (Luke 10:27).

It is not only individuals who fail to do what God wants. Institutions and corporate bodies also fail. They fail to operate with truth and integrity. They fail to act with justice and fairness. They fail, in other words, to live by those values that in the corporate world reflect love. There is corporate, as well as individual, sin.

Love and obedience

If, then, we are to live more fully in the way God wants us to live – to live in obedience to his will, there appears to be a simple answer: love more. Love is of God, who is love. He initiates love. If we love it is because he first loved us (1 John 4:19). So to be a loving person is to be one who is responding more and more to the gift of God that is offered to them, available to them. Given our suspicion, if not actual scepticism about authority these days, talk about obedience can feel to some people an erosion of their personal freedom, especially if obedience is emphasised as a required aspect of personal spirituality. Talk of 'submission' is even more problematic. It feels too passive and has nuances of a child submitting to a Victorian father, a slave submitting to a master, a conquered people submitting to an invading despot. The more we rightly emphasise the worth and value of an individual, not least in the sight of God, the more we can feel uneasy about an attitude of submission.

Once again we have to remind ourselves that Jesus' prayer begins with the loving Fatherhood of God. The will of God and obedience (even submission) have to be understood in this context. Jesus' experience in the Garden of Gethsemane as recorded in the Gospels again reminds us of the way obedience is played out, not least at the most difficult of times. Love can be very challenging on occasions. Obedience may not be comfortable – it certainly wasn't for Jesus – but it may be the only way that the loving purposes of God can be realised. This is obedience for our ultimate good, not because God demands it to satisfy some kind of despotic whim or to gratify the desire for power, but because love requires it.

Obedience to God's will is neither a matter of ticking boxes nor of servile submission, but of entering more and more into a relationship with God as loving Father, so that we are clearer about what God wants of us and more able to carry that out. This is the work of God's Spirit in us as both guide and enabler, and prayer is one of the ways that relationship can be helped to grow and deepen.

PART B

Flat-packed furniture can be a nightmare to put together. Domestic peace in not a few homes has been broken by a husband and wife attempting to build a wardrobe. It's not just that the instruction booklets never seem to be quite as straightforward as they claim. Communication between the couple can become a little strained. We've no doubt all heard the exasperated cry, 'Just tell me what you want me to do and I'll do it!' Oh that it was that easy!

Discerning God's will

We can sometimes feel like that with God. We want to do his will, if only he would make it plain just what he wants. Generalities like, 'Be loving', 'Don't tell lies', 'Go the extra mile', are all right as far as they go, but the trouble comes when we get down to specifics. We'd like God to be in the detail, not the devil. Some clarity would help.

Of course, there are times when what God wants feels very clear, and then it is a matter of how willing we are to be obedient. But often, discerning God's will is less clear, and it can occupy a considerable amount of our prayer time.

For many years my work involved discerning people's vocation to the priesthood. By its very nature, what I was doing, together with the candidates, was trying to discover what it was exactly that God was calling them to. It wasn't just a matter of agreeing with what they felt. We needed to be clear-minded about what the task of a priest would require of them, and to be clear-minded about what gifts, personality, experience and abilities they would bring to that calling. There were interviews, there were the views of other people, there was the candidate's own sense of calling, and there was prayer, seeking for the guidance of the Spirit as we sought to come to a decision. Even then we didn't always get it right.

How do you seek to discern God's will for you? Do you depend on your own feelings, conscience? Do you find the Bible a help? Do you seek the help of other people?

Listening

It reminds us that one of the most important things in prayer is not talking but listening. Although some people say they experience an actual 'voice', for most of us God speaks in a rather less tangible way. Either way, to 'hear' God we need to be quiet, to be focused, to be receptive.

Some people find silence not only difficult to find but difficult to cope with. A busy household, rushing off to work, people always around you, someone always playing music. Quiet can be in short supply. Your house might not be the place to find it. It might be in the garden, in a local church (which is why they should be left open), just sitting in the car. There is no 'proper' place in which to pray.

There's also the quiet 'within'. Finding a quiet spot can suddenly make the noise of all the thoughts rushing around inside one's head all the louder. They can be very insistent. It's not usually much help to try to force them to be quiet. Get yourself comfortable, relax any uptight muscles, breathe slowly and try to let all those thoughts clamouring for attention drift into the background by focusing on something that draws your attention to God. It may feel strange the first time you try. But persevere. It takes practise.

We may even fear the silence. It's not just thoughts about all the chores, what to buy your cousin for her birthday, how to face the boss with the latest sales figures, that churn around. Much darker thoughts can suddenly rush in. They may be thoughts that we have been avoiding for a long time – anxieties, guilt, doubts. How we might deal with them is a whole book on its own, but enough to say that simply running away from them by filling the silence with chatter is not a long-term solution. Here, as in all aspects of prayer, God's Spirit is there to help us. We should not be reluctant to ask for his help.

Where is your 'quiet place'? Do you find silence a joy or a trial? Do you ever ask the Holy Spirit to help you in your praying?

Discerning God's will is one thing; obeying it can sometimes be a very different matter – not because we don't want to be obedient but because what we feel God is asking of us is so contrary to what we had expected, or is so demanding of us. We may not see the point in being called to a certain action. Only time can tell. And if you find that you have made a mistake in what you thought God was asking of you, don't be too hard on yourself. God understands. Discernment is an art, not a science. It emerges from our relationship with God, and with the best will in the world we don't always get it right.

SIX

On Earth as in Heaven

PART A
Heaven
In the popular view, heaven is a blissful setting where all is sweetness and light. A favourite holiday spot with great company, nice food and a good drink may be 'heaven'. When listening to a wonderful and moving piece of music a person might say they have 'gone to heaven'. But for the most part it is only when we die that it is thought we have the chance to go to heaven. And then it's only if we have been good. Quite what it will be like is far from certain. Sitting on a damp cloud with endless harp music would hardly add up to an eternity of happiness! Most people hope heaven is where they will meet up with loved ones. It's where relatives who have passed on are sitting watching us and over us. Bubba Watson, the American golfer, has talked about his father watching him from heaven. Other sports people raise their eyes and hands to the skies in an act of dedicating their efforts to their mother or father or coach or hero, 'up there in heaven'.

Personally, I am very cautious about heaven. Not that I don't believe there is life after we die, nor even because I have no certainty that it is where I shall end up! I just don't find the usual descriptions of heaven very helpful.

A matter of justice
In popular Christian apologetics, one of the reasons given for why there must be life after this one and therefore a heaven is based on a question of justice: life on earth for so many people is just plainly unfair. Heaven balances this out. If there is any justice to be had and if there is a just and loving God then what is so blatantly unjust here must be put right

after we die. It is a view that has sustained many people amid the grim realities of their life on earth. Heaven is the place of it being 'all right'. All the horrors, the violence, the brevity, the suffering of this world are absent. Heaven is a place of peace and light, where there is no sorrow, no pain, no parting. It is where lost partners and loved ones are found once more, where parents are reunited with children they lost too young. A place of love. A heavenly paradise. For very understandable reasons we project on to 'heaven' all that we hope for, all that we long for, all that will put right what feels wrong now.

Jesus' view

This is, of course, to have a view of heaven that starts with us and what we want it to be like. But if we start with just one clue from something Jesus said, we have a slightly different picture. It occurs in a conversation Jesus had with some Sadducees. Among other things, they did not believe in a life after death, and so they presented Jesus with what seemed like an impossible situation as a way of showing the illogicality of believing in a 'heaven' after this life. They set out a hypothetical situation based on the custom whereby if a man's married brother died, he was expected to marry the widow. So what would be the situation, they asked, if there were seven brothers and one after another six of them died, each having married the same woman, and none of them had any children? Whose wife would she be in heaven? Jesus' reply cuts the ground from under their feet by suggesting a quite different view of heaven: 'When they rise from the dead, they neither marry nor are given in marriage, but are like angels in heaven' (Mark 12:18-25). Just what the relationship between the woman and the men will be in heaven is not made clear, but it is implied that it will not be the same as on earth. For some people, that would make heaven less than they hope for.

God's abode

All that we say about heaven is in some sense conjecture, a series of pictures trying to give us an idea about what is in fact a mystery. The simplest thing to be said may be that heaven is where God is. The Scriptures see heaven as where God lives. It's his abode (Deuteronomy 26:15). He is not there alone. Angels are said to be with God, worshipping him (Nehemiah 9:6). To be in God's presence is to be in heaven. Heaven is where God is and where God is recognised as God, the loving Father. To be in God's presence and to reject God might be one way of defining hell.

Apparently, even angels have the freedom to make a choice to reject God, as the story of the rebellious angel tells us. Satan is the figure that came to stand for a total rebellion against God. While in the Old Testament he is sometimes included among the heavenly host and as, at worst, a Tempter (Job 1:6), later developments picture him as at war with God and finally thrown out of the heavenly realm along with those who had sided with him (Luke 10:18).

Positive responding to God means not only worship but obedience. If the way of the loving Father is a way that makes for fullness of life, that life is most fully experienced in heaven where what God lovingly wills is responded to and realised.

It is perhaps in this way that we can understand what it means for God's will to be done in heaven, where there is perfection of love and also the full realisation of what God wills and desires.

It is this that the Lord's Prayer seeks for in our life here on earth. Whatever the critics might say about Christianity being all about 'pie in the sky when we die', it is in fact a very down-to-earth religion. That way of life that we have suggested characterises life in 'heaven' needs to be 'earthed', needs to be followed in the everyday actions, choices and decisions of life here on earth. Otherwise it remains an out-of-touch piety.

The everyday

Religion is certainly about more than just our everyday concerns, but it is certainly not about less. There are those who seek to live out the spiritual life by withdrawing from the day-to-day confusion and tangled complexities of worldly activity, but that is not how the majority of us can or desire to live. A religion that is only for the pious few is not what Jesus taught and lived. It is amid the joys and pleasures, the fears and griefs of life that we are called to love God and love neighbour. It is not simply what we do in church or in our times of prayer that reveals how far we are following God's will. It is in the way we behave at work and at home, in public places and in private, in our business dealings and in our leisure, that we are called to show that obedient response to what God asks of us. Christian obedience must not be pigeon-holed into that area of our life we label 'religious'. It concerns all of life – all of our life as individuals and all of our life as members of society. That is why Christianity cannot ignore politics or questions of social justice. As the old slogan used to say, 'All of life is here.'

Obedience

We tend to think of obedience as a matter of submission to authority – whether that be of an adult over a child, the authority of the boss over an employee, or the authority of the police and the government. It's a matter of doing things the way we are told to. A matter of keeping the rules. And of course there are plenty of 'rules' when it comes to religion, and Christianity is no exception. But rules and commands are a second-best. They are necessary given the way human beings are. They seek to prevent chaos, anarchy and injustice. At best they seek to promote well-being and good order. But authority and obedience don't have to be seen in the context of rules. They can also be seen in terms of love. In this context the authority of a loving Father is an authority built on a mutually loving relationship, not on rules. Obedience to what a loving father desires for a child is a response not of duty but of love.

God the loving Father looks for this response from his children. That is not what we actually see 'on earth', although that is, presumably, what it is like in heaven. At best, our loving response is partial. At worst, it doesn't get off the starting line. When we pray the prayer Jesus taught us we are calling upon God to help change this situation. We want him to make a difference. But the prayer also challenges we who pray it to check just how loving our response is to what we understand God's will to be for us. To behave on earth as those in heaven behave is a high aspiration. But it is not impossible, certainly not impossible to take seriously and work on. Humanity is not a 'hopeless case'. Certainly not when seen from God's perspective. However, realisation of the loving purposes of God on earth can only be achieved in terms of a fully loving relationship in which the love, mercy, grace and power that God offers are received and responded to.

Love and justice

When we talk of loving fathers and children, it is possible to conclude that all that is involved here are individual relationships, the way an individual responds to the love of God. That is not the case. There is also the social context. In the history of the Hebrews there were, of course, highly significant individuals whose relationship with God made huge differences. Yet the overall emphasis is not upon individuals but upon the whole 'people of God' and the way the people as a whole responded to God. In Christianity, especially in the Protestant tradition, the individual's response to God is seen as very important, but the context is still the whole Body of Christ. There is a corporate as well as an individual responsibility both within the life of the Church and in wider society. It is there that all that we understand in terms of love in individual relationships become issues of justice. The loving Father is also a just God, calling us to act justly as well as lovingly so that life on earth more closely mirrors life in heaven.

The failure of the Church to act justly and with integrity, be that at the local level of congregation or more widely, is a scandal. When it becomes public it is not simply an embarrassment but also reveals a fundamental failure to live up to the values of the Gospel, of the kingdom and of God. Among the most notorious and the most damaging in recent years have been the instances of child abuse. The perpetrators may have been individuals, but the response of Church authorities far too often has been evasive or worse. Rather than a loving and just response to the plight of the victims, there have been cover-ups and a corporate defensiveness that exacerbated the situation. Too many people are having to live with the consequences of both the initial trauma and the failure of the Church to act justly.

There is corporate greed as well as individual greed – greed for wealth, greed for power. In his letter to the Colossians, Paul described it as a form of idolatry (Colossians 3:5), for it becomes an alternative 'god'. It leads to actions that erode human rights (think of bad employment practices), have far-reaching and sometimes devastating consequences across the world (think of financial malpractice), and which are ecologically damaging (think of what is happening to the world's rainforests). The very sustainability of the earth is put at risk. To act in accordance with God's purposes and will is not just a matter of individual response but a matter of global significance. There is such a thing as corporate responsibility as well as individual, and there is a distinct dynamic that occurs in corporate decision making that is not simply a sum of individual choices. The Church, although itself tarnished, has a responsibility to speak out and act in the face of injustice – doing so in the name of a loving God who is Father of all people.

PART B

My father was not a great churchgoer. He said he had been to church enough as a child. As a member of the choir he attended at least twice every Sunday. He had a gentle suspicion of anything that smacked of too much piety and was heard on more than one occasion quoting an old saying: 'Don't be so heavenly minded that you are of no earthly good.'

Heaven and earth

Earthiness is part and parcel of the Christian religion. Jesus demonstrated that God is very down to earth as well as being a heavenly Father. Our prayers and our spiritual growth need to be 'earthed'. That is not at all the same as saying that there is not a proper place for those aspects of prayer which help our hearts and minds and souls soar above and beyond our everyday concerns. We need to raise our attention above the mundane horizon to contemplate the possibilities and realities that are present with God. Meditation can help us to grow in our perception of the lordship and holiness of God and what his call to us to be holy might mean.

Thoughts of heaven may be important to ensure that we aspire to grow in faith, in love and in reverence, but we are not to neglect the reality of the world around us.

At one level, this has a very practical implication for our praying.

Spend a few moments reflecting on where and when you most often pray. Do you have a specific prayer time or is it done all in a bit of a rush? Is it last minute or planned? Is it when you feel fresh or at the fag-end of the day?

This is not to suggest that there are only 'right' times to pray, but we can get into habits of prayer that end up making prayer a matter of when it is convenient for us rather than how it best helps our relationship with God.

Being quiet

We have already looked in chapter 3 at how it can be helpful to find places where we can be quiet. Jesus suggested we should go into the privacy of our own room to pray. His concern was not directly about being quiet but about not using prayer in public as a way of showing off how religious we are. His point was aimed at the Pharisees. But it does underline the fact that where as well as how we pray is significant.

Over the years a number of people have told me that they pray as they drive to work. I have to say that worries me, but that is more a matter of safety than of spirituality.

Just as ultimately there is no 'right' place for prayer, nor is there a 'right' posture. Traditionally, kneeling has been felt to be most appropriate, the physical position reflecting the desired humble approach to God. But standing, sitting and lying prostrate all have their place. Being uncomfortable for the sake of it has never seemed to me to be very helpful. Painful knees or a crick in the neck is not likely to help prayerful attention.

Commonly it is suggested that we sit, not slouch, in a way that holds the body still and upright without being rigid. Indeed, we should be relaxed, and there are ways to help us take the tension out of our bodies. Consciously going from head to toe and relaxing the muscles and the tension as we go is one way. Some people find it is helpful to close their eyes; others prefer to focus on a particular object – a candle or picture. Try to breathe slowly.

> Try a different setting and posture to the one you normally use for your prayer. Do it often enough to get rid of the simple feeling of strangeness. Does it make any difference to the way you pray?

Awareness of our own physicality may well feature occasionally in our prayers, not least if it gives rise to thankfulness for health or recovery from illness, or petition in times of sickness or distress. Our own well-being may give us cause to reflect on those with impaired abilities and our attitudes to those we see as 'disabled', either physically, mentally or socially.

Stewards

The 'earthiness' of our faith reminds us that in thanking God for the beauty, wonders and mysteries of creation we have a responsibility as stewards of the earth. Concerns about climate change may draw our attention to the increasing vulnerability some places experience from either the lack of rain or from deluge and flood. Our prayers for those who suffer from famine on the one hand and from the destruction of their property and livelihoods on the other, should lead us to consider to what extent we are contributing, even in a small way, to the perils of our planet by our lifestyle.

Consider whether there are any changes you might make, in what you buy or in what you do, that could enhance your good stewardship of the earth.

"Our Earth needs constant concern and attention. Each of us has a personal responsibility to care for creation, this precious gift which God has entrusted to us." *Pope Francis in a speech to the European Parliament in Strasburg, November 2014*

Jesus's resurrection is the beginning of God's new project not to snatch people away from earth to heaven but to colonize earth with the life of heaven. That, after all, is what the Lord's Prayer is about.

N. T. Wright[4]

---

4. N. T. Wright, *Surprised by Hope* (SPCK, 2007).

SEVEN

Give Us This Day Our Daily Bread

PART A

Many years ago I spent a month at St George's College in Jerusalem taking part in a course on archaeology and the Bible. As well as looking at famous sites in and around Jerusalem and visiting Bethlehem and Galilee, we also spent some days and nights in the Sinai desert. It was mid August and during the day extremely hot. I was not used to it, and moving around was exhausting. At night it was very cold and difficult to keep warm. During those few days, in quite a stark way, I began to see the difference between wants and needs. Standing in the sun at two o'clock in the afternoon at an ancient crossing point in the desert listening to a lecture on origins of language and the earliest forms of dwelling, it felt a struggle just to breathe and keep going. It wasn't easy to take in what was being said. The plastic flask of tepid water was not what I wanted but it was very much what I needed – two litres of it an hour to keep me from dehydrating. I was lucky that I didn't have to go hunting for it.

Needs and wants

In situations where people face the daily struggle just to survive, the insatiable desire of wants just doesn't appear over the horizon. It is enough if the basic needs can be met, even partially. But for many people in the affluent developed world the clear distinction between need and want is blurred. It is largely assumed that needs are provided for. What keeps the standard of living and the economy ticking over is not the meeting of needs but the constant demand of wants. If it falters, the advertisers are always on hand to tickle our fancy, appeal to our love of the novel, boost our sense of status, ensure we do not fall behind the pace. Suitably stimulated, we then go out and buy more 'stuff'. We are conned, very subtly and often subconsciously, into thinking that what we want is in fact what we need. I understand that it is now possible to purchase a scarf that changes colour according to the heat of the body. It costs about £750. Who on earth would want one? Certainly no one needs such a thing. But no doubt they will sell.

It would be very easy to be 'high-minded' about this, to pretend we are not like that, that in fact we rather scorn this chasing after 'stuff'. We may have read James Wallman's book *Stuffocation* and are attracted by his warnings about the continual acquisition of possessions.[5] While there are indeed some people who by choice or by necessity do live in a way that others would consider to be austere if not downright monastic, the majority of us go along with the chasing after 'stuff' to a lesser or greater extent. We very much benefit from this capitalist system that requires the cycle of stimulating wants and meeting their demand, and we play our own small part in the process. To put it bluntly, this is currently the only economic show in town. That it creates wealth and encourages invention and new technologies is generally accepted to be a good thing. But this same system also creates disproportionate and growing differences between the rich and the poor, and can encourage the exploitation and abuse of work forces. It is not a universally fair or just system, although it could be argued that without the encouragement of 'wants', the meeting of needs would be even more difficult.

Basic needs

The plain fact is that if our basic needs are not met, we are in a very sorry state indeed. It is shocking to know that about one in nine people in our world, nearly 800 million, do not have enough to eat to keep them healthy.[6] A United Nations survey in 2005 indicated that 100 million people were homeless and 1.6 billion had inadequate housing. It is notoriously difficult to obtain accurate figures for homelessness in the

---

5. James Wallman, *Stuffocation: Living More With Less* (Crux Publishing, 2013).
6. World Hunger Statistics.

United Kingdom, partly because a considerable amount of the problem is hidden and partly because definitions vary. In June 2016, Crisis (a charity concerned with homelessness) reported that in England more than 8000 people were sleeping rough in London alone. In 2016, 57,750 homeless households across the country met the strict criteria required by local authorities to house them, and more than a quarter of a million asked for homelessness assistance.[7] All these figures have seen an increase over previous years. In 2016, the United Refugee Agency recorded that more than 21 million people are refugees, and in total three times that number have been forced from their homes.[8]

This little excursion into economics is not an attempt to condemn the fact that most of us have plenty of things we want as well as need. Living a full life is not the same as merely surviving, and it involves more than meeting our most basic requirements of food, shelter and clothing. It's all a bit more complex than the simplistic distinction between never having enough to meet all our wants and only having enough to meet our basic needs.

More than survival

It remains true that if our basic physical needs are not met, survival is difficult if not impossible. But if we are to do more than simply survive, there are other needs that have to be satisfied. To be fully healthy human beings, food, clothing and shelter alone are not enough. There are also significant emotional, mental and spiritual needs. They are not the icing on the cake, nor an occasional extravagance. They are there in the very way we grow into and maintain our humanity, and while high culture and advanced technology may be their products they are not dependent upon either. Indeed, it could be argued that the apparently simpler, though not necessarily less sophisticated, cultures and communities are better at meeting some of these needs than modern, so-called advanced societies.

---

7. Statistics from www.crisis.org.uk (accessed 29 November 2016).
8. Information from www.unhcr.org (accessed 29 November 2016).

Most of us have experienced times when there just seems to be too much going on around us – too much activity, too many sounds, too much noise. Just too much of everything. We feel overwhelmed by it and need a break, some peace and quiet. Our digital age bombards us, and a survey carried out in the summer of 2016 by Ofcom revealed the fact that people are now seeking 'digital detox' – a break from their tablets and smartphones. Just switching off. Many schools offer their pupils the opportunity to be quiet, to have a time-out to just be and reflect. Retreats are a common feature of many religions as part of a person's spiritual well-being. We need quiet to 'gather ourselves'.

The flip side of this is the fact that we also need stimulation. While short periods of sensory deprivation may be helpful for relaxation and meditation and can be used therapeutically, long-term deprivation is damaging, and can result in hallucinations, anxiety and depression. It has sometimes been used as a form of torture. Our brains work better and are less likely to fall victim to certain forms of dementia if they are stimulated. Varied mental stimulation actually increases the cell connectors in our brains (the dendritic branches) and helps improve thinking and memory.

Emotional needs

We also have emotional needs, such as the need to feel loved, to feel valued, to feel capable, to feel secure. When these needs are met we experience a sense of satisfaction or contentment, created by the release of certain chemicals. But without these good feelings not only do our lives feel dull and lacking in meaning, but we also become vulnerable to emotional problems such as depression and anxiety, and even to addictive behaviour.

Since the 1970s, psychologists and educationalists have identified what is called 'emotional resilience' – the capacity to respond positively to change and stress, to adversity and disaster. Among the things that help build up such resilience are the presence of a supportive network of friends and family; nurturing a sense of self-worth; having goals and plans to achieve them; keeping things in perspective; self-awareness of how one is feeling; a healthy lifestyle. Resilience helps to combat the destructive effects of stress – a feature that is increasingly common in the workplace. The Health and Safety Executive reported that in 2014–15 the total number of cases in Great Britain of work-related stress, depression or anxiety was 440,000, with 9.9million working days lost. Stress is most common in public service industries such as education, health and social care.[9] It is suggested that the current generation of teenagers are less emotionally resilient than their parents, and cognitive behaviour therapists, for example, expect an upturn in the number of people seeking help for stress-related disorders. In a world where change occurs at an increasing rate and stress is a frequent experience, the need for emotional resilience could well be seen as a basic need to help ensure our well-being.

Meeting physical, mental and emotional needs is necessary for our personal healthiness. It is true too of spiritual needs. Howard Clinebell, an American Methodist minister and professor of pastoral psychology, identified a number of spiritual needs, or hungers. Among them were:

- Love, from others, the self and an ultimate source;

- Vital beliefs that lend meaning and hope amid tragedy or failure;

- Inner wisdom and creativity;

- A sense of oneness with other people and the natural world;

- The resources to help heal guilt, resentment, shame and to deepen trust, self-esteem and a love of life.[10]

In themselves, these spiritual needs and the well-being that arises from their being met are not tied to any one religion. They are common to the human condition in which we are understood to be spiritual as well as physical, mental and emotional beings. However, we could put

---

9. Information from www.hse.gov.uk (accessed 29 November 2016).
10. http://www.takingcharge.csh.umn.edu (accessed 29 November 2016).

them into a specifically Christian context and see how the Christian faith seeks to meet these needs.

The teaching that God is himself love and that Jesus calls us to love God, and others as oneself, is at the heart of the faith. A personal relationship with this God through Christ and in the power of the Spirit offers the opportunity to draw upon the resources that provide the vision, hope, worth and spiritual resilience not only to meet what life throws at us but also to grow in that fullness of life Jesus spoke of. A God who values us, whose promises are trustworthy, who forgives us and transforms us, whose Spirit brings healing and wholeness is a God who makes available those resources our spirits need. And we can draw upon them through prayer, through meditation and through fellowship with other believers.

This day

All this leads me to suggest that when we pray, 'Give us this day our daily bread,' we are in fact asking God to meet this whole range of our daily needs of body, mind and spirit. 'This day' reminds us that what we are asking for is not an abundance beyond our needs but sufficient for each day. In our dependence on God we live 'day by day'. It recalls the story of the manna in the wilderness when God provided the Israelites with food so that they would not starve in the austerity of the desert. Those who collected more than they needed discovered that it went rotten and stank (Exodus 16:1-30). God not only taught his people that he was a God who cared for them and met their needs, a God to be trusted, he also taught them not to be greedy or to doubt his care for them.

However, there is an additional complication. While it is clear what 'Give us this day' means, it is not so obvious what 'daily' bread means. The word used for 'daily', *epiousios* in the Greek, appears nowhere else in Greek literature and is therefore something of a mystery word, and it is therefore even more difficult to know what Aramaic word Jesus would have used, for which this is a translation. Even the second-century

Christian writer Origen had never come across the word. Discoveries to help solve the puzzle came from such diverse places as the caves of Qumran and the ruins of Pompeii. Scholars have pieced together clues from an ancient set of accounts in the everyday Greek of the people of New Testament times and the Latin of a wall inscription regarding a soldier's daily rations, and suggest that the word most probably meant 'the coming day' or 'tomorrow'. A note in the New English Bible suggests 'our bread for the morrow', and a similar note in the New Revised Standard Version has 'our bread for tomorrow'. William Barclay, in his translation, suggests 'our bread for the coming day'. This suggests that the prayer is asking that there will be sufficient rations in the house overnight for the needs of the next day. We are asking that in our task as followers of Jesus we will have the provisions, the resources we need not only to be the people God wants us to be but also to do the tasks we are called to undertake.

According to John, Jesus identified himself as the true 'bread from heaven', the one on whom we feed and grow into that fullness of humanity which is God's desire for us (John 6:35-59). In some traditions this has been linked with the Body of Christ in the bread of the Eucharist and the receiving of the sacrament each day.

Meeting our needs

A prayer that asks God to provide our needs on a daily basis inevitably raises the question about how we understand God might do this. Where there is no shortage to meet our daily needs the simple answer is that God just does, the evidence is there in the provision made: crops grow, houses are built, people are kept safe and grow up in loving relationships. The appropriate response, it can be argued, is not one of endless questioning about how but of an attitude of thanksgiving for the fact that God does provide. But what if this is not the case? What do we make of those who starve, are homeless or are oppressed by violence? Does God not care for them? Is there a hidden favouritism in his providing? Or perhaps he does care for all but is unable to carry out what his love would want?

The questions are as old as the hills and continue to test the minds of theologians and the faith of ordinary folk. I can only offer the way I have come to view this. In his wisdom, God has decided not to use arbitrary power but to involve us in a joint enterprise so that the prayer to God for our daily needs is also a challenge to us to play our responsible part in ensuring that the daily needs of all are met. In a world where resources are not available in equal measure, the challenge is for us to ensure that there is an equitable distribution. In striving to do that we grow in our exercise of our responsibility. We grow in that outward-looking concern which at the personal level is love and at the social level is justice. The world is such that there are droughts and there are gluts, there are areas of peace and areas of violence. Both nature and the action of people make this an uneven world, but it is the context in which humanity has been set and in which we are called to learn what it is to be responsible and loving people, growing in the likeness of God's model of what we should be like – Jesus.

This is no simple answer, and it is certainly no short-term solution. Humanity is slow to learn, and a step forward in one generation can slip back in another. It is not easy for those who suffer to have to face the fact that God takes a long-term view, that he invites and encourages us but does not coerce us – not even into goodness. The freedom God has given us comes at a heavy cost that is borne unevenly. But to love us means giving us that freedom – to respond or not. And God in Christ has himself known the cost of what that freedom can do. As individuals, and collectively as communities and nations, we are called to work with God in whatever ways we can to meet the daily needs, not just of ourselves and those we love but of all.

PART B
Want and need

The shop was crowded and above the noise came the plaintive wail of a young child, 'But I want it.'

The mother's exasperated response could also be heard, 'But you've got one already, and in any case I'm not buying anything else today.'

For my last birthday my two children bought me a sports car. It took me some time to get over the shock. 'You always said you wished you had one,' they said, 'so here it is.' It's 'toys for the boys', and, in my case, an old boy. The reality is I don't need it. I already have a perfectly good car that gets me and my wife around. But I love the sports car. Could I do without it? Of course I could!

In a world of finite resources we do well to stop occasionally and reflect on all the 'stuff' we have.

Spend five minutes sitting in a room in your house – any room. Look around you. What five things in the room would you find it difficult to do without? What five things could you easily do without?

We sometimes imagine that it is our possessions that bring us happiness. Some of them may certainly do that, but we can unconsciously come to assume that more and more possessions would make us even happier, and that is seldom true.

Make a short list (ten items) of what gives you the greatest happiness. How many of these involve people and how many are objects?

Downsizing your house can be a joy ('Thank goodness we got rid of all that clutter') or a painful process of making choices, deciding priorities, especially when it comes to objects that are not simply functional but have a host of memories associated with them ('It felt like giving part of my life away').

Simplicity

Most of us have more than we need because basic needs alone can make for a rather bleak life. But that is the reality for too many people, and in a world of finite resources there comes a point when my having more can mean someone else has less. It is what led Mahatma Gandhi to say,

'I live simply so that others may simply live.' The practical reality of that was obvious in India; it is less obvious in the affluent West. If we are at all sensitive to the needs of those in other countries who have next to nothing and who struggle daily simply to live, we will include them in our prayers. It is sometimes much more difficult to know what we should do as a result of our concern and our prayers. Giving to appropriate charities can be one way, but you may have thought of others.

When Jesus included the request to God to supply our daily bread, he was thinking about needs, not luxury. But while 'bread' suggests physical needs, we actually have others needs as well if we are to be mature and live what Jesus would call an abundant life (John 10:10).

What do you consider to be your basic needs? Do you have all that you need? What makes for abundant living?

Dependence

Our prayer asks God to supply those needs, and as our needs are met we might rightly want to thank God. We may well believe that ultimately 'all things come from you, O God', but there are many others also involved. At Harvest Festivals we focus our thanksgiving not only upon God but also upon farmers and producers, packers and transporters, processors and retailers. Without them we know we would not have 'our daily bread'. In an age when being independent and self-reliant is considered a virtue, we do well to remember just how many others we are actually dependent upon even for our most basic needs.

Alongside our intercession for God to meet our needs and the needs of others there should be thanksgiving for all involved in meeting those needs and upon whom we depend.

For the fruits of his creation,
thanks be to God;
for his gifts to every nation,
thanks be to God;

for the ploughing, sowing, reaping,
silent growth while we are sleeping,
future needs in earth's safe keeping,
thanks be to God.

In the just reward of labour,
God's will is done;
in the help we give our neighbour,
God's will is done;
in our world-wide task of caring,
for the hungry and despairing,
in the harvests we are sharing,
God's will is done.

For the harvests of the Spirit,
thanks be to God;
for the good we all inherit,
thanks be to God;
for the wonders that astound us,
for the truths that still confound us,
most of all, that love has found us,
thanks be to God.

Fred Pratt Green (1903–2000)

EIGHT

Forgive Us Our Trespasses

PART A

There is nothing particularly religious about the idea that as human beings we make mistakes, get things wrong, hurt other people, fail to show the care we know we should. Unless we are social and moral anarchists, we recognise the practical reality of the law and of morality. People break the law and offend moral codes. The secularist may insist that both are subject to change and context and that neither are universal nor absolute, but they wouldn't thereby deny their importance. A failure to comply with either code creates a degree of fracture in personal relationships and in social cohesion. The question is then a matter of what to do about it. At one extreme there is retributive punishment or revenge, and at the other there is the blind eye. Between them lie restorative justice, transformation and forgiveness. The offender may or may not feel remorse, shame or guilt. And that will not necessarily depend on the seriousness of the offence. A murderer may show no sense that he has done anything wrong. A petty thief may be haunted by guilt. For one person, 'getting away with it' may be what they aim for. For another, only admitting the wrong can make things right for them.

Hierarchy of wrong

While we commonly agree that wrong is wrong even though we might disagree on exactly what we mean by the word, it is generally acknowledged that there is a kind of hierarchy of wrongdoing. Crimes are petty or serious, moral lapses are outrageous or trivial. Tax evasion has almost become the thing to do among some groups of people rather than the thing to avoid, and certainly it's not seen as being as objectionable as a mugging. Exceeding the speed limit by a few miles an hour is viewed very differently to dangerous drunken driving. Damage to property is considered less heinous than violence to a person. It is when people are involved that we feel something is particularly wrong. In most cases of wrongdoing there are in fact implications for others even if there is no immediate victim. Embezzlement might appear to be simply a crime against the organisation or system, but in practice it will make its mark on the lives of others.

There are times when what is otherwise agreed to be wrong is felt to be justified. A lie may be an offence against truth but it may also be a kindness towards another person. 'White' lies often fall into this category. If the law is broken in the course of a protest against injustice or the erosion of civil liberty there may still be considerable sympathy for the law-breakers, especially when it occurs in countries where other forms of democratic protest are limited.

Different cultures can have very different codes of behaviour and social taboos. At the current time these are perhaps most obvious in attitudes towards the place of women in a society, affecting what they may or may not do, what they wear, what choice they have in deciding whom they should marry. For one culture a punishment regime may appear quite normal and necessary to ensure social standards, while for another it is viewed as brutal and inhumane. Where cultural norms are backed up and justified by religious faith they usually become universalised and made absolute. Thus for many Christians the Ten Commandments are not seen simply as a set of rules governed by their particular context in time and culture but are the rules for all people whether or not they recognise the God whose commands they are. Those who seek to create a world caliphate would have a similar attitude to the law set out by Islam. In practice, neither all Christians nor all Muslims agree on the exact requirements of the law of God as understood by their religion, and over the centuries this has all too often led to division and violence.

What we do, and the norms governing what we do, matter. Breaking those norms is significant for individuals and for society because it puts relationships and social well-being at risk. Breaking the rules God has established threatens the relationship not only with other people but, more importantly, with God. And this is what this part of Jesus' prayer is about.

Textual differences

Over the centuries, the precise wording of this section of the Lord's Prayer has differed in the various translations. Indeed, some of that difference appears in the original Greek, as can be seen when one compares Matthew's version of the Lord's prayer with Luke's. Matthew (Matthew 6:12) uses the word *opheilemata* (debt) and *aphes* (release or cancel). Luke (Luke 11:4) uses *hamartia* (sin) but also *aphes* (release or cancel).

A comparison of various translations reflects this difference:

Matthew 6:12:

> Forgive us our debts, as we forgive our debtors
> (King James Version)

> Forgive us the wrong we have done as we forgive those who have wronged us (New English Bible)

> Forgive us our debts, as we ourselves have forgiven our debtors (NRSVA)

> Forgive us our failures in our duty to you as we have forgiven those who have failed in their duty to us (William Barclay)

> Let us off our debts just as we have let off all our debtors (Nicholas King)

Luke 11:4:

> Forgive us our sins; for we also forgive everyone that is indebted to us (King James Version)

> Forgive us our sins for we too forgave all who've done us wrong (New English Bible)

Forgive us our sins, for we ourselves forgive everyone indebted to us (NRSV)

Forgive us our sins as we too forgive everyone who fails in his duty to us (William Barclay)

Forgive us our sins for we ourselves also forgive everyone who is in debt to us (Nicholas King)

Forgive us our trespasses as we forgive them that trespass against us (*Book of Common Prayer*)

Forgive us our trespasses as we forgive those who trespass against us (*Roman Catholic Missal*)

Forgive us our sins as we forgive those who sin against us (*Common Worship*)

This comparison reveals a number of different words used for the 'wrong' for which forgiveness is asked: debt, wrong, failure in duty, sin, trespass. We will explore three of these in more detail.

Debt

Debt, we are told by the anthropologist David Graeber, was the origin of trade nearly 3000 years before the invention of coinage.[11] Goods were handed over with the promise that a 'repayment' would be made at some point in the future. The word, which is thus grounded in the world of commercial transactions, can also be a metaphor for anything that is owed by one person to another – for example, a debt of honour, a debt of gratitude, a debt of duty.

To pay a debt is both a moral and legal obligation, and failure to meet a debt could result in shame, a fine or imprisonment. The most famous and oldest British debtors' prison was the Clink, with its debtors' entrance in Stoney Street, Southwark, and it was originally the prison owned by the Bishop of Winchester whose London palace was nearby.

---

11. David Graeber, *Debt, The First 5000 Years* (Melville House publishing, 2011).

It gave rise to two slang expressions: 'in the clink' for being in prison, and 'stony broke' meaning having no money. Being in a debtors' prison did not of itself cancel the debt, which still had to be paid either by what could be earned from work in the prison or through the generosity of a relative or patron. It was only in 1970 that imprisonment for debt was removed from the statute book.

The Old Testament taught that debts owed to a fellow Israelite were to be cancelled every seven years (Deuteronomy 15), but nevertheless, the failure to pay a debt could result in the debtor becoming a slave of the person to whom the debt was owed. This was still the case in Jesus' time, as we can see from the parable he told concerning the king and his servants. One of them owed the king 10,000 talents, and because he could not pay, the king ordered that he, his wife and his children should be sold (Matthew 18:25). However, so long as they were Israelites, such slaves would be freed in the year of Jubilee, and their debts would be cancelled (Leviticus 25). Graeber says that the word 'freedom' originally meant 'freedom from debt', and was only later extended to mean being free from any kind of constraint.

It is not only individuals who can incur debt. Nations can too, either through extraordinary expenditure as in times of war or through an imbalance of imports over exports. A healthy economy can live with such debts because those to whom the debt is owed trust that loans and interest on the debt can be repaid. However, where a country's economy is in a critical state, debts pile up with little hope of repayment and the country can become financially unviable. Concern for developing countries who found themselves in such situations led in the 1990s to the Jubilee 2000 campaign, its name indicating that it drew upon the principle of Jubilee in the Old Testament. Demonstrations at the G8 meeting in Birmingham in 1998 led to debt relief being taken very seriously by the international community. The Heavily Indebted Poor Countries Initiative was set up to provide debt relief for the poorest countries. Conditions were set to the way the programme worked, seeking to ensure that the money saved would be used to reduce poverty and to enforce structural reforms in the countries' economies. The nature of these conditions led to considerable criticism of the programme from some quarters where it was argued that it actually widened the gap between the rich and the poor and increased the dependence of poor countries upon the richer ones. Nevertheless, the programme was further extended in 2005 at the Gleneagles meeting of the G8 to offer 100 per cent cancellation of multilateral debts.

Debt in a secular setting is reasonably clear, but what does it mean to be in debt to God? C. F. Evans, in his commentary on Luke,[12] suggests that we fall into debt by neglect of God's commandments. It was a very Jewish way of understanding the nature of sin and has a legal connotation. In his letter to the Colossians, Paul wrote of God's forgiveness as 'erasing the record that stood against us with its legal demands' (Colossians 2:14). The record he refers to (in Greek, *cheirographon*) was a handwritten promissory note which was legally binding. We owe God obedience, and when we fail to be fully obedient we fail to fulfil our obligation and hence fall into debt. St Anselm saw the debt as one of honour.[13] Through our wrongdoing we fail to show God his due honour and thereby incur a debt of honour. Christ, by his death, went beyond what mere duty demanded and therefore his surplus of honour, as it were, makes up for our deficit. The debt of honour has been paid.

Trespasses

As a child I remember going into a private wood where there was a big notice saying, 'Trespassers will be prosecuted'. I don't think I knew exactly what the notice meant, only that I shouldn't be there. The strands of barbed wire round the notice may have given me the clue. Climbing the gate and entering the wood felt quite daring and not a little scary. I wasn't there very long and I'm not at all sure why I wanted to be there in the first place. I was only about seven at the time. But that's the trouble with being told not to do something: it increases the appeal and the excitement of actually doing it!

---

12. C. F. Evans, *St Luke* (SCM Press, 1990), p.483.
13. St Anselm, *Cur Deus Homo I.xi.*

Trespass has the normal meaning of crossing a boundary into a forbidden territory, be it a wood, a home, a country. In more legal language it is 'unauthorised entry onto another's soil'. The law also recognises trespass to the person, which includes assault, battery and unlawful imprisonment, and trespass to possessions (chattels), which in recent years has been used to settle disputes concerning unsolicited bulk emails.

The Greek word that is normally translated as 'trespass' is *paraptoma*, and while it does not occur in the Lord's Prayer, it does in Paul's letter (Ephesians 2:1 and Colossians 2:13). It is possible that a distinction was made between trespasses, which were wrongs committed by the people of God, and sins, which was the term used for wrongs committed by Gentiles. We have noted that 'trespass' is the word preferred by the liturgists. Its literal meaning is 'a fall away from being close', and in moral terms means a lapse or error, including those that are unintended. In a relationship with God, a 'trespasser' falls away both from God's law and from walking close to God.

Sin

In old English the word *syn* had the general sense of wrongdoing or misdeed and was used to translate the Hebrew word *chata* and the Greek word *hamartia*. Both of these words are associated with missing the mark, the one in archery and the other in spear throwing.

A miss, they say, is as good as a mile. In other words, a miss is a miss whether it's by a small amount or by a large one. There may be mitigating circumstances: an archer, for example, may miss the bullseye by a fraction because a sudden gust of wind takes the arrow off target. But it's still a miss, and that's what is shown on the scorecard.

The same might be said about sin: sin is sin whether it is a big sin or a small one. This is the position taken by most churches, the issue then being whether or not the sin has been repented of. In the Catholic tradition, however, a distinction is made between 'mortal' and 'venial' sin. The latter is considered to be less serious and does not result in a complete separation from God and eternal damnation, which is the consequence of an unrepented 'mortal' sin. To decide whether a sin is venial or mortal, the following three questions need to be considered:

- Does it involve a grave matter?
- Did the person commit the sin knowing it to be both sinful and grave?
- Was the sinful action done deliberately and with the person's full consent?

The Catholic Catechism of 1858 offers this explanation of what is meant by 'grave':

Grave matter is specified by the Ten Commandments, corresponding to the answer of Jesus to the rich young man: 'Do not kill, Do not commit adultery, Do not steal, Do not bear false witness, Do not defraud, Honour your father and your mother.' The gravity of sins is more or less great: murder is graver than theft. One must also take into account who is wronged: violence against parents is in itself graver than violence against a stranger.

A list of mortal sins includes such matters as abortion, adultery, apostasy, blasphemy, contraception, euthanasia, incest, pornography and rape.

Grave or not, sin makes a break in one's relationship with God. While repentance shows the sinner's willingness to have the relationship mended, only the grace of God can create and restore a living relationship between the penitent and God.

As we saw above, the notion of 'missing the mark' lies behind the Greek word for sin, and this deserves further consideration. While there is room for discussion about the relative gravity of 'missing the mark' by a large or small distance, there is the assumption that we are all in fact aiming in the right direction – i.e. trying to 'hit the target' of God's law, of righteous living.

But there is sin that feels rather different. It's as though we miss the mark not by aiming at the right target and shooting wide, but by aiming at the wrong target entirely. Those whom we might describe as 'evil' appear by their actions not to be aiming at goodness at all but in a completely different direction. What they aim for is nothing like the action desired by God or shown to us in Christ. They may believe they are acting to achieve a good, but it is such a distorted understanding that their 'good' is what we would describe as 'evil'. Events in recent years relating to extremist terrorist groups, to child abuse, to mass killings give us plenty of examples of this. All too tragically the perpetrators may very well hit the target they are aiming at – but in the light of Christ it's the wrong target.

There is also, of course, the failure to hit the target simply because we never even shot the arrow! We mostly think of sin as wrong action, but there is also sin which is a failure to act at all. The technical term for this is 'sins of omission', contrasted with action sins which are 'sins of commission'. The priest who simply passed by on the other side when he saw the robbed and beaten traveller lying by the side of the road may have been worried about action which would have resulted in ritual defilement, but his failure to act compassionately was a sin – a failure in love (Luke 10:25-37).

Sins of omission are in many ways the more hidden sins – less obvious and public. Yet they can be just as damaging. The guilt felt for not having done something when in our heart we knew we should have can be just as powerful as committing a bad action. We only have to consider what a grieving relative can go through when their failure to act had a direct consequence in the death of a loved one. And it doesn't have to be as dramatic and tragic as that. The trouble is that we can so easily justify our not doing things – we were too busy, it would have been embarrassing, we don't know what good we would have done anyway, we just didn't think it was important. The harsh fact is that in response to God's call to all of us to act lovingly to him, to others and to ourselves, any failure to love is a sin – whether that be by our action or by our inaction.

Sin, then, occurs in our failure to act perfectly. We try our very best but seldom, if ever, get things totally right. At one level this might appear to be a very pessimistic view of human nature, yet it is nevertheless supported by everyday experience. In spite of our best endeavours we just don't get it right, and we can all echo St Paul's words: 'For I do not do the good I want, but the evil I do not want is what I do' (Romans 7:19). He put it down to the 'sin that dwells within me' (Roman 7:20).

Why do we do wrong?

Theologians have argued about what it is that makes us behave in this way. Some have suggested that it is a flaw in our human nature while others have gone further to say it is much more serious and that we suffer from 'total depravity', which affects even our freedom to make choices. St Paul was the first to explain that the fault can be traced to Adam and Eve's disobedience in the Garden of Eden. He saw a solidarity of sin: 'sin came into the world through one man, and death came through sin, and so death spread to all because all have sinned' (Romans 5:12). Christian orthodoxy insists that our sinful tendency is inherited; it is part of our nature and not, as Pelagius suggested, merely learnt by following Adam's bad example. The original act of disobedience changed human nature from the perfection created by God to one that is now 'tainted' by sin. All humanity shares in Adam's guilt, and only Christ's redeeming death is able to make the difference. As St Paul says, 'as all die in Adam, so all will be made alive in Christ (1 Corinthians 15:22). The solidarity in Adam created a sinful humanity; the solidarity in Christ produces a redeemed humanity.

Whether or not we feel convinced by the arguments about 'original sin', the Christian tradition overall provides a realistic view of humanity which includes its propensity to do wrong, and a hope that believes in God's transforming promise for us all.

Forgiveness

This hope arises from the possibility of forgiveness. Sin prevents us from fulfilling that honouring of God's name (being) and looking for the coming of God's kingdom which appeared in the early part of the Lord's Prayer. If those sections of the prayer are to be said with integrity and in good faith, then something needs to be done about those aspects of our lives that set up a barrier to their realisation. We cannot ourselves pay off the debt nor mend the fracture caused by sin. We cannot 'earn' our way back into God's good books. We can only ask for forgiveness and place ourselves into the hands of a merciful, loving Father God. So Jesus' prayer brings us to the request for forgiveness.

Although we can do nothing to earn forgiveness, it does not mean there is nothing we can do to make forgiveness a reality in our lives and not just a promise and a hope set out by God before us. The request for forgiveness is itself grounded in the realisation that through what we have done, or what we have omitted to do, we have acted wrongly. This is the first step along the road to forgiveness. If we don't admit we've gone wrong in some way, forgiveness remains a gift on offer but one we see as having no relevance to us. Private, sacramental or general confession is the recognition that there is something in our lives that actually needs forgiveness. And when we do admit our faults, God responds with forgiveness. Indeed, it is the prior promise of forgiveness that may be the very thing that encourages us to admit our faults in the first place.

In one of his letters St John says, 'If we confess our sins, he who is faithful and just will forgive us our sins and cleanse us from all unrighteousness' (1 John 1:9). Admitting we have done something wrong is a major step along the path to forgiveness. A necessary step but, it's not the whole journey. 'Just saying sorry isn't enough,' my mother used to say. 'You've got to mean it.' And part of 'meaning it' is the intention not to do it again. Forgiveness isn't a slot machine that issues a pardon when you insert the 'confession' token, leaving you free to go and do whatever you like again. Where there has been actual hurt to a person or damage to another's property, some act of reparation may be a clear and explicit way of giving meaning to an admission of wrongdoing and a request for forgiveness. Such a reparation is not 'purchasing' forgiveness but a significant symbol of the recognition of being in the wrong and seeking to make amends, seeking to heal the relationship the wrong damaged.

God's forgiveness is a gift, but it has a cost. We may feel it is costly for us to drum up the courage to admit we have done something wrong, but forgiveness has a greater cost. And this for me has been the key to my understanding of what occurred on and through the cross. For me, the death of Christ is not a *price* he had to pay in order to satisfy the holiness or the honour of God who could then forgive. The cross is the terrible sign of the *cost* God experiences in forgiving – a forgiveness that is and was always on offer. The cost of forgiveness is all the greater because of the hurt our sin does to him, the holy God, the pain of our failures to live up to the purpose God has for us to be freely responsible, loving people.

We only have to think of what it can cost us to forgive someone who has really hurt us – or perhaps even more, when they have hurt someone we love. We marvel at the courage and the personal cost of those who have suffered appalling loss and destruction through the actions of others, be they abusers, fraudsters or madmen with guns, and who can still forgive. It is very understandable when families come out of court and speak of their pain caused by the person just convicted of a terrible crime against them and who tell reporters, 'We've got justice now but we can never forgive him for what he did.' Deeply understandable, but not the costly way Christ calls us to. Those who are able to stand amid the devastation to their lives and say, 'I forgive,' are the ones who show the better way. Theirs is the way of hope and strength, but it comes at a cost.

An example

There are many inspiring examples of forgiveness, some of them consciously following Christ's way, others not. Here is an extract from a blog of just one: Chai Ling, the founder of 'All Girls Allowed',[14] who as a student saw the destruction and death of Tiananmen Square in 1989:

Two decades ago, the Chinese government's crackdown in Tiananmen Square left hundreds of my fellow students dead . . .

To me it seems like just yesterday. I began that day with great hope and anticipation for a new China, but it ended as a day of unspeakable sorrow. Now, 23 years have passed . . .

There could only be two futures for China: an outcome of continued fear, or a destiny that opens the door to true freedom — and forgiveness . . .

It is painful for me to remember what happened on that June 4th, 1989, when I witnessed the death of a dream. I still mourn for what 'could have been.' And for a long time, I battled bitterness and anger whenever I thought of the leaders who chose to take a path of destruction that day . . .

But then I was confronted with the example of Jesus. He loved women, children, the poor and the oppressed in a way that was radically countercultural – and he called me to do the same.

He also forgave the very people who ridiculed him and nailed him to a cross: 'Father, forgive them, for they know not what they do. (Luke 23:34)

And again, he called me to do the same.

Because of Jesus, I forgive them.[15]

The Greek word which is normally translated as 'forgiveness' is *aphesis*, and it has the meaning of 'a letting go, sending away, release from debt or obligation, pardon, complete forgiveness'. In Matthew's version of the Lord's Prayer it is forgiveness for debt, but in Luke's version it is forgiveness for sin.

---

14. 'All Girls Allowed seeks to restore the God-given life, value and dignity to women by seeking transformation both of hearts and of societies.' See http://www.allgirlsallowed.org/about/who-we-are for more details (accessed 5 December 2016).
15. Chai Ling, '"I Forgive Them": On the 23rd Anniversary of the Tiananmen Square Massacre in 1989', 4 June 2012. Available at: http://www.huffingtonpost.com/chai-ling/tiananmen-china_b_1565235.html (accessed 1 December 2016).

Release from debt

The most obvious way to get rid of a debt is to pay it off. This is what mortgage payments are doing, the payments continuing until the whole debt, plus interest, has been met. But payment is not always easy. Circumstances can change and repayments may not be met. Mortgage companies know of this possibility and they have arrangements in place by which to repossess the house and meet what is owed. The debt is paid, but the person's situation may end up being desperate as a result. There is a more compassionate, but less commercially acceptable, solution to solving a debt problem – writing it off. Family members or friends may do this even if it results in making sacrifices themselves. Although financial debt can cause considerable problems, it is reasonably easy to quantify the debt and to know when the debt has been met.

Other kinds of debt are not so obvious. As I write this, the 2016 Rio Olympics are coming to a conclusion. Great Britain has enjoyed considerable success and there have been frequent interviews with successful competitors. Many of them speak of the debt they owe to their coaches, their teammates, their families and friends. It's a debt that may involve some money, but is much more in terms of support and encouragement, of time and motivation. 'I did it for them,' is a phrase often used, and the implication is that all the effort put in on the track, in the pool or in the gymnasium is a way of showing appreciation for what is owed and a way of meeting the debt. There is no exact equivalence in such circumstances yet it feels very real. It is part of what makes relationships special, a way of saying that what is done is not taken for granted. Children often speak of the debt they owe to their parents, a debt they know they can never pay. But the way they live and the way they bring up their own children in some way seeks to show that the debt is not forgotten. Ultimately, the debt of love can never be met, and parents who constantly remind their children just how much they are owed are more likely to build up resentment and guilt rather than gratitude and love.

Being in debt to someone means that we have to a greater or lesser extent put ourselves into their power. How that power is then used makes all the difference. One of the problems associated with payday lenders is that their initial offer of a loan looks like a relief from the power of a current debt, but borrowers all too often find themselves ever more imprisoned in the cycle of high interest rates, further debt, requiring more loans and getting more and more in the grip of the lenders. If someone then were to come along and pay the debt it would indeed feel like a release, a freeing, a letting go.

All these everyday examples of debt and how it may be met, or not, are clues to the way we can understand what it means to be 'in debt' to God and how our debt to him is met.

But there are major differences. The harsh reality is that no matter what we do, our debt to God cannot be paid – not by us. We cannot earn our way out of it; we have no assets sufficient to meet the debt; we cannot bribe our way out of it. We are in God's hands, in his power. It is the nature of that power that makes all the difference. The only power God knows is 'love' – it's what he is, it's what he does. Love seeks in any and every circumstance to find a way to enhance the long-term well-being of the beloved, not to diminish it. Love does not seek to drive the person in debt into ever greater depths of debt. God seeks to release us from our debts, to pardon us, to forgive us. And as we have seen, that has a cost that he is willing to pay – for our sakes and for the sake of love.

Forgiveness of sin

Forgiveness is neither forgetfulness nor is it collusion. God does not ignore the reality of sin or 'debt'. Holiness does not pretend an evil is anything but evil. Forgiveness is not an attitude of 'never mind'. If we have hurt someone, have lied, have cheated, have failed to be compassionate, what we have done does matter. We should mind. What we need is not forgetfulness but forgiveness.

Whether God forgets or not, the fact is that we do forget trivial wrongs against us. They were too small a matter to be too upset about.

We shrug and move on. But some things are too significant to be forgotten. The consequences may live on in the lives of others all too obviously. A careless moment of lack of concentration may result in the death of a child in a road accident. That isn't something that can be forgotten. The family has to live with that loss all their lives – and the driver has to live with the knowledge of what was done all their life.

Forgiveness doesn't say it didn't happen but that, terrible as it was, it will not become the cause of hatred, resentment, bitterness, estrangement. Forgiveness seeks to break the cycle that revenge can create. It looks to restore a relationship that wrongdoing can fracture and tear apart. It seeks to transform a tragic situation not only for the sake of the perpetrator but also for the sake of the victim. People forgive, painfully and sincerely, even in the most terrible situations where there has been torture, abuse or killing. They do so as an act of love towards the other but also as an act of love towards themselves, for by forgiving they choose not to participate in the same attitudes and actions of wrong and evil. Forgiveness not only breaks the cycle of wrong; it also has the power to transform. God's loving forgiveness seeks to do that, and in his love and through his Spirit he has the power to bring about transformation. It is God's gracious, merciful, transforming forgiveness that we ask for as we repeat this section of the Lord's Prayer.

All that has been said to this point emphasises the willingness of God to forgive us, the way we can appropriate that forgiveness and the call for us to be forgiving people. But what are we to make of the fact that Jesus spoke of a sin that could not be forgiven?

'I tell you, people will be forgiven for every sin and blasphemy, but blasphemy against the Spirit will not be forgiven. Whoever speaks a word against the Son of Man will be forgiven, but whoever speaks against the Holy Spirit will not be forgiven, either in this age or in the age to come'   *Matthew 12:31, 32*

It looks here at last as though we have hit the 'bottom line', the point where God's willingness to forgive gives out. Is this really such a heinous sin that it falls beyond the pale of God's love. To help us, we need to remember that this saying comes just after an altercation with the Pharisees (Matthew 12:22-4). Jesus had healed a demoniac who was blind and mute and the crowds were amazed, declaring that Jesus must be the 'Son of David' – the one promised to bring in God's kingdom. But when the Pharisees heard about it they wrote the miracle off, saying that this fellow Jesus had cast out demons by the power of the chief of demons, Beelzebul. In other words, having been presented with an act of God's kingdom, his healing power, they dismissed it as being an act of Satan. Jesus had understood himself to have acted under the power of the Holy Spirit. The Pharisees were saying white is black, good is evil. If you are this spiritually blind, Jesus says, you have actually taken yourself beyond the point where you are able to receive forgiveness, no matter how much it is offered.

As we forgive

We have noted on a number of occasions that there is no way we can earn forgiveness. We cannot pay the debt we owe; we cannot right the wrong we have done. God's forgiveness is an act of grace, a gift. But are there any conditions attached to the gift? There are plenty of churches that have been offered gifts of money on the condition that it is spent on the organ or a flower stand. Conditions may be attached to legacies, sometimes to ensure the money is spent wisely, sometimes as an act of power beyond the grave. Does God set conditions for forgiveness?

The request for forgiveness is the only part of the Lord's Prayer that has a qualification attached to it. The force of that qualification is not immediately obvious. At first sight it looks like a condition: Forgive us our sins, as we forgive those who sin against us/Forgive us our debts, as we also have forgiven our debtors. Does this imply that God's forgiveness is dependent upon us being forgiving? Are we asking God to forgive us our sins *because* we forgive others? While such a condition is not found in Jewish liturgical prayer, there is evidence of this belief in the book of Ecclesiasticus (Sirach) in the Apocrypha: 'Forgive your neighbour the wrong he has done, and then your sins will be pardoned when you pray . . . If someone has no mercy towards another like himself, can he then seek pardon for his own sins?' (Ecclesiasticus 28:2, 4). It is possible that Matthew was interpreting the phrase in this way (see Matthew 6:14, 15). A more natural understanding of the Greek *hos kai* ('as also') would be to see it as a way of establishing a similarity between God's forgiveness and ours, or possibly as an encouragement to imitation (cf Matthew 18:33). Luke's version (*kai gar auto*, 'for also we') looks as though it is a modification of the original version that Matthew records, and Evans suggests that this means:

> A direct request for forgiveness can be made by those who, as disciples of Jesus, are already in the position of having forgiven others or of habitually doing so. They are already living the life of the kingdom and reproducing the character of the Father and it is for the Father to follow suit.[16]

While God does not place conditions on the offer of his forgiveness, there are conditions upon which our receiving forgiveness depend. We have seen already that the request for forgiveness can only arise out of a recognition that there is something that needs forgiving and for which we ask for forgiveness. There is also a challenge here: that we who are forgiven should be forgiving in the same way as God forgives. This may be reasonably easy over small matters, but even then we can fail, forgetting just how much we ourselves have been forgiven. Jesus talked about this in the parable of the king who wished to settle accounts with his slaves (Matthew 18:23-35). It appears immediately after Peter's question about how often we should forgive someone. He thought seven times was pushing it, but Jesus told him he should forgive without limit: 'seventy times seven' (Matthew 18:21, 22).

---

16. C. F. Evans, *Saint Luke*, p. 483.

Forgiveness lies at the heart of the Good News for a 'fallen' humanity. It mends what is broken, it restores what is damaged, it heals what is wounded, it pardons what is owed. It is the very nature of God to forgive, and as we ask to be forgiven we are reminded that we, too, are challenged to be forgiving. This is the way of Christ.

PART B
Approaching God

As a youngster I remember being told by my teacher to fetch a book from the headmaster. I went to the head's room and walked in to get the book. I was told quite sharply that this wasn't the way to do things. 'You don't just barge in', he told me. 'You knock and wait to be told to enter.' Things have changed these days with open-door policies, but most of us recognise that there are appropriate and inappropriate ways of approaching others.

God, we might say, operates an open-door policy. He doesn't shut himself away behind a closed door. Although there is a tradition which says we make our prayers 'through Jesus Christ our Lord', God doesn't require us to go through a whole array of hoops to reach him. There will be many occasions when we talk with God unannounced, as it were.

Confession

Public worship, especially when there is a formal liturgy, usually has a pattern that recognises that for our sake, if not for God's, there are ways we should prepare ourselves to enter the presence of God. So, in common with the pattern of the Lord's Prayer, we begin with focusing on God through hymns and prayers of praise. We then move to confession, admitting that in contrast to this holy God whose praise we have just been proclaiming, we are sinners. As the words of a prayer in the Communion Service say, 'We do not presume' to make our way into God's presence. We come admitting we have no rights, no deserts, but confessing those things we have done wrong or the good we have failed to do. In one form or another we then hear the assurance of God's forgiveness. So it is as forgiven sinners that we make our approach.

Do you find the pattern of praise and confession followed in public worship helpful for your private prayer? Some people use **ACTS** as a way to shape their prayers: **A**doration; **C**onfession; **T**hanksgiving; **S**upplication.

Confession is not 'grovelling'; it is an act of facing the reality of what we are and what we do that is less than God asks of us. That can be challenging, especially in our private acts of confession when we are admitting to particular wrongs and not merely joining other worshippers in a 'general confession'. It challenges our honesty. We are usually more inclined to admit to minor wrongs and less willing to face things that are more serious. Or we can be so concerned by what we see as a particular wickedness that we forget everything else.

The assurance of forgiveness

In public worship or in confession to a priest we have the assurance of hearing God's forgiveness. When we confess in the course of private prayers, there is not that kind of assurance. Some people use a sentence from the Scriptures to give them a clear reminder of God's forgiveness – for example, 'If we confess our sins, he who is faithful and just will forgive us our sins and cleanse us from all unrighteousness' (1 John 1:9).

In your private prayers of confession, what do you find assures you of God's forgiveness?

Being assured of God's gift of forgiveness is important in preventing us from becoming obsessed with what we have done wrong. It can feel rather annoying if someone constantly comes up to us asking us to forgive them for a wrong done ages ago and for which we have made it clear we forgive them. God doesn't get annoyed if we constantly confess the same wrong, but he does want us to know the release that forgiveness offered and received gives. Confession and forgiveness allow us to move on. It can be transforming.

Forgiving others

Our willingness to forgive those who have hurt us is important for them, but also for us. Unforgiven sin is imprisoning both for the perpetrator and for the victim. That doesn't mean it is always easy to forgive someone who has hurt us. It can feel easier just to bear a grudge. But it is important to remember that it is primarily forgiveness of the person who has done something wrong and not simply forgiveness of the wrong itself. Confession and forgiveness have more to do with relationships than with rule books. To forgive someone means that we value the relationship more than the action that caused the hurt.

> Spend some time reflecting on whether there are hurts in your life that have remained unresolved, relationships that even if not broken are distorted by resentments or grudges. How might forgiveness be offered?

Sin is a breaking of the right order of things – the moral order, the legal order, the spiritual order. Forgiveness restores that order. But sin is most importantly a breaking of the good order of relationships – with God, with others, with ourselves. Forgiveness is a restoration of harmony, of peace, of love. It is a sacrament of reconciliation, restoration and transformation.

> As well as asking God for forgiveness and offering forgiveness to others, do you ever consider there might be things for which you have to forgive yourself?

Thanksgiving

Because forgiveness is costly and restored relationships are a blessing, being forgiven should lead us to thanksgiving – most importantly thanksgiving for all that Christ did in bearing the cost of forgiveness. Forgiveness does not come cheap, and it lies at the very heart of the gospel and the story of Jesus, not least his death.

The Lord is merciful and gracious,
slow to anger and abounding in steadfast love.
He will not always accuse,
nor will he keep his anger for ever.
He does not deal with us according to our sins,
nor repay us according to our iniquities.
For as the heavens are high above the earth,
so great is his steadfast love towards those who fear him;
as far as the east is from the west,
so far he removes our transgressions from us.
As a father has compassion for his children,
so the Lord has compassion for those who fear him.
For he knows how we were made;
he remembers that we are dust.

Psalm 103:8-14

The saying is sure and worthy of full acceptance, that Christ Jesus
came into the world to save sinners.   *1 Timothy 1:15*

NINE

And Lead Us Not Into Temptation

PART A

Beverly was tired of her father for ever moaning about her friends. It didn't seem to matter who she was going out with, he would have something to complain about. They were too loud, he didn't like the clothes they wore, one of them was covered with tattoos. For goodness sake! 'They'll lead you astray,' he'd warn her. 'I know you – you are easily led and there are all sorts of temptations in the places you go.' What was he on about?

Fathers worry about their kids, perhaps especially their daughters. It goes with the territory of being a loving dad, even if it can feel over the top and desperately old-fashioned. But it would be much more disturbing if parents purposely put temptation in the way of their children. The dad who takes his son on a poaching trip. A mum who suggests a daughter slips a bottle of perfume into her pocket when she next goes shopping. In big and small ways there is no doubt that it happens. But it is not good.

Does God tempt us?

So this section of the Lord's Prayer has a strange feel to it. Why on earth would God, the loving Father, even want to 'lead us into temptation'? Are we asking here for escape from something that it would not even have occurred to God to do? If the God we are addressing is indeed the loving Father that Jesus has spoken of and who is addressed right at the beginning of the prayer, can we really imagine that he would want to set the direction for our lives which would lead to temptation? He is well aware of how liable we are to get things wrong, so surely he wouldn't just add to the problem? The prayer doesn't simply ask God to help us not fall into temptation, but that he should not take an active part in leading us along that path.

The implication of this, that God could be the author of temptation, seems to have caused problems from the outset. In Luke this is the final petition in the Lord's Prayer, and it is possible that Matthew added the next phrase, 'but deliver us from evil', to establish the fact that evil in fact does not come from God but from the 'evil one'. In the letter of James, the author explicitly says, 'No one, when tempted, should say, "I am being tempted by God"; for God cannot be tempted by evil and he himself tempts no one' (James 1:13).

Early commentators like Dionysius, Tertullian and Cyprian put glosses on the phrase so that it could be understood to mean, 'do not let us be led into temptation', or 'do not suffer us to be led into temptation.' Reference was made to 1 Corinthians 10:13 which says, 'No testing has overtaken you that is not common to everyone. God is faithful, and he will not let you be tested beyond your strength, but with the testing he will also provide the way out so that you may be able to endure it.' This led some of the Latin Fathers to suggest it means that we are not to be led into temptation that we cannot bear.

Are such interpretations legitimate – do they reflect the way Jesus would have understood the words he taught? Or are they a way of dodging a difficult saying? Preachers are known to be selective in their choice of texts, especially when not following a lectionary, so that they can avoid those passages they don't agree with or which they find difficult. No doubt we all have our favourite passages and sayings and we tend to skip over the ones that appear to contradict our understanding, even though we know that wrestling with difficult texts can lead us to deeper insights.

While all translation is to some extent an act of interpretation, there have to be some guiding principles to ensure that such interpretation is neither arbitrary nor simply convenient. One such principle is to test the interpretation of a particular passage or saying against the overall picture one has of God or of Christ. That is not to say that there is no room for surprises, but rather to try to ensure that there are not straight contradictions and radical inconsistencies. Simplistically, does the interpretation here chime in with the overall picture we are given in Scripture?

We need to be constantly reminding ourselves that Jesus was a Jew and that although he brought new emphases and understandings and insights into the Jewish tradition, his general way of thinking was inevitably shaped by his Jewish upbringing at home and in the synagogue. The scholar Joachim Jeremias suggested that Jesus may well have known and used an ancient Jewish evening prayer which included these words:

> Lead my foot not into the power of sin,
> and bring me not into the power of iniquity,
> and not into the power of temptation,
> and not into the power of anything shameful.

We should note that this prayer, as in the phrase we are considering, makes its request as a negative. 'Lead us not into temptation' is the only petition in the Lord's prayer that has such a negative. This Jewish prayer is understood to be asking God not to let these things happen. They are not asking God not to do them.[17] This would mean that in the Lord's Prayer we are asking not to be allowed to be overpowered by the testing power of temptation.

Test

The association with 'testing' is not arbitrary. The Greek word which is normally translated in the Lord's Prayer as 'temptation' also had the meaning of trial, or test. In the NRSVA, the translation of both Matthew 6:13 and Luke 11:4 is, 'Do not bring us to the time of trial.' 'Lead us not into temptation' is put into a footnote as an alternative. The translators have decided to be very specific in this notion of test or

---

17. Joachim Jeremias, *The Prayers of Jesus* (SCM Press, 1967), pp.82-104.

trial, indicating that what Jesus was referring to was that time of testing and tribulation that it was believed would proceed the arrival of the end of the current age. The petition thus becomes a request to shorten that period. Such a time was understood, slightly ambiguously, as the work of Satan but permitted by God who was also asked to shorten the period of tribulation. Jews believed that if such a period of tribulation were to last for very long, then even the righteous would fall. Hence the request for it to be shortened.

The time of trial may, on the other hand, not refer to the tribulations expected before the last days but the very present trials that had been experienced by the Jews in the centuries immediately before the coming of Christ and that were to be experienced by the early Church. There was the ongoing pressure on Jews and then Christians to give up their faith. There was persecution; there was the threat of death. Here was a testing that no one wanted to have to face. It was a perfectly understandable and reasonable request to ask God to keep them from such times. Jesus himself made such a request in the Garden of Gethsemane, although he would face it should it come.

In a more general sense, we might understand this petition as asking God not to put our loyalty and obedience to the test because we cannot be sure we will be able to meet what is asked of us – although see 1 Corinthians 10:13 quoted above. Such a request seems perfectly understandable.

Challenges

We do not want to be led into temptation, nor do we want to have to face a test that could break us. Both can be dangerous for our well-being. But neither temptation nor testing is necessarily entirely negative. It may be one thing to criticise a father who sets up physical tests that he knows a child will fail because he believes 'it will do him good to be broken'. But to cushion a child from all challenges is not a loving way to help that child grow and develop. In big and small ways we all have to face things that test our courage, our integrity, our mental abilities. We grow by facing them and finding ways to tackle them. Success boosts our confidence, and learning how to handle failure is a major lesson in growing up. It is similar when it comes to spiritual and moral tests (temptations): it is only by facing them that we grow in wisdom and tenacity to overcome them. We may well need help from others and from God. Their care for us is shown in giving us the help we need, just as we should help those we care about.

Is there challenge in this petition or is it just a longing to be 'let off lightly', either from difficult times that will test our character or from temptations that will test our spirit and faith? The challenge comes in the knowledge that while God will be with us in whatever we face, he doesn't simply magic difficulties away. As a loving Father he knows what is helpful to our growing into the people he longs for us to be. Some of those things may be tough to face and even tougher to endure. At times there seems to be an arbitrariness and unfairness about what some people have to face while others appear to sail through life untroubled. This disparity itself presents us with a challenge – not to be resentful if we are the ones who have difficult times, and not to be complacent if life treats us well.

PART B

'The easiest way to deal with temptation is to give into it.' People say that as a joke as they take the third piece of delicious chocolate cake. It covers their sense of doing something they know they shouldn't. Everything is easy to resist except temptation, although there are plenty of websites that will help you try.

Temptations

Some temptations are common to most of us – the temptation to tell a lie, for example. But many of the most difficult are specific to our nature or to our circumstances. I have never been tempted to produce fraudulent company accounts, but then I don't have anything to do with accounts. But I do have a car, and I am sometimes tempted to drive too fast.

Are you aware of anything that you find particularly tempting and difficult to resist? What do you do about it? Does praying help?

For some people, giving way to what tempts them is a slippery slope that has damaging consequences – one only has to think of alcohol or gambling or overeating. Sometimes we can be all too ready to condemn such people, not knowing just how hard they may have tried to overcome their temptation.

In asking God to help you to overcome your temptations, do you ever ask him to help others to overcome their temptations?

Testing

It is suggested that temptation may be better understood as 'test'. A temptation tests how committed we are to the truth, to being non-racist, to honesty. There is also the testing of our faith. The force of certain arguments may test our faith. Tragic events either to ourselves or to others may test our trust in the loving God. When prayer feels futile and God seems very distant we can be tempted to give up. What then should we pray? Should we pray that we can avoid listening to arguments that question our faith? Should we give way to despair amid tragedy? Should we avoid the struggle with doubt by denying our faith? We will not always be able to avoid such testing situations. But we can ask God to help us face them and to remain with us even when we feel he is far away.

If you have had to face a situation through which your faith was tested, what helped you get through? Have you ever been asked for help from someone for whom a testing situation broke their faith?

Do you see a test as a challenge or as something to dread? Can you point to a time of testing that helped to strengthen your faith and love for God?

Persecution

In this country, faith is increasingly seen as an irrelevance, and to admit to being a Christian can sometimes feel embarrassing. We might be ridiculed, but we are not very likely to experience actual persecution. That is not the case in an increasing number of areas of the world. Christians lose their jobs, have their churches destroyed, can be imprisoned or even killed.

Do you ever feel embarrassed in talking about your faith? Do you remember those Christians in other parts of the world who suffer persecution?

To encourage us in our lives and in our faith we are sometimes advised not to think of things as difficulties but only as opportunities, not as obstacles but only as challenges. As we use the Lord's Prayer, we can ask God to help us to see things in this way. We can grow spiritually as well as in maturity by grasping opportunities and facing challenges. We pray that neither will be so testing that they 'break us'.

TEN

But Deliver Us From Evil

PART A

Every now and again, tabloid headlines scream out the word **EVIL**. Such headlines attract and repel us at the same time. They are dramatic, and there is a kind of trembling fascination in the appalling events that lie behind them. We want to know, yet at the same time we fear what will be revealed. What most of these headlines point to is the potential in human beings for such wickedness that only this worst of words, 'evil', is sufficient.

'Evil Isis groomers condemned' was a headline in the *Manchester Evening News* on 15 June 2015.

'Trapped in a web by evil monsters' was a headline quote from a girl kept in slavery, cited in the *Sunday Express* on 24 November 2013.

Is evil real?

Few people deny the reality of evil. Almost daily, from somewhere in the world comes news of such appalling, destructive behaviour that the only way we can describe it is to call it 'evil'. One-off bad actions may occasionally be described in this way, but to call a person 'evil' means that they are persistent in what they do. Hitler, Stalin and Pol Pot were evil. So were Peter Sutcliffe and Fred and Rosemary West. Evil may become institutionalised, as it did in the machinery of the Holocaust, but it was people and their repeated evil choices that made it happen.

It raises the question as to whether natural forces can appropriately be called 'evil'. An earthquake, a volcano or a tsunami may be incredibly threatening and devastating for property and people's lives. But as natural forces they have no power to make choices, no freedom of will that could have made them different. Their effect may be made all the worse by bad decisions about where housing is located and what emergency help was available, but in themselves such natural events are not evil, no matter how much suffering they cause. They are morally neutral.

This, of course, is largely a modern view. In the past, such events had personality projected on to them to help explain them and their terrible consequences. In a lesser way, this persists by giving storms and hurricanes names. In 2015, the UK Meteorological Office introduced its 'Name our Storms' project, beginning with Abigail on 10 November. Events, too, can be personalised through identifying them with an individual character, sometimes mythological, as in this headline:

'Racially motivated graffiti' on Polish club as Brexit 'lets evil genie out of the bottle'   *Daily Mirror*, 26 June 2016

A battle?

This is not the same, however, as saying that evil is directed or initiated by a personal evil force, comparable in some way to God. For millennia, human beings have sought to understand the universal experience of good and evil, their origins and their effects. In Hinduism, Taoism and Buddhism, evil is seen as having no ultimate reality. With its associated suffering, evil is the result of ignorance or of the persistent illusion of the existence of a personal self. In religions where there is a dualistic understanding of ultimate reality, such as in Zoroastrianism and Gnosticism, two eternally co-existent deities were believed to be engaged in an endless battle between good and evil.

This has sometimes mistakenly been thought to be the Christian position, with God and the devil battling it out. But there is a significant difference. Christianity, like Judaism and Islam, are unambiguously monotheistic: they believe that there is only one eternal God. Whatever else exists does so as part of his creation, never as an equal deity. So clear was Isaiah about this that he was led to put it in a very dramatic way. It resulted in a saying that on the surface might make it look as though God does indeed create evil:

I form light and create darkness,
I make weal and create woe;
I the Lord do all these things.

Isaiah 45:7

To Isaiah, and to the Hebrew viewpoint in general, distinctions that would intrigue later philosophers had no place here. The demand of a clear monotheism made it necessary to say that everything was in the power of God, including those trials and tribulations that were the result of human freedom of choice, or that were brought upon them by the judgement of God. Isaiah was thinking about the Exile, a time of very considerable physical and spiritual difficulty that was interpreted as being the consequence of Israel's failure to follow God's teaching.

At a personal level, we all know that there is a struggle that goes on inside us between the good we know we should do and the wrong that we are tempted to do. So strong can this struggle feel that it may be described as a battle or as a war. At a personal level, it reflects the greater struggle that involves God as he fights against evil.

The evil one

This leads us, however, into another area where opinions have differed over the centuries and is a debate to which our current phrase from the Lord's Prayer has contributed. In its liturgical form, such as in the *Book of Common Prayer*, in *Common Worship* and the *New Roman Catholic Missal*, the phrase is, 'deliver us from *evil*', and this is the same for most translations of the Bible. Some, however, have this: 'rescue us from *the evil one*' (NRSVA), or 'deliver us from *the Evil One*' (Nicholas King). Are we then talking of 'evil' as an abstract force or trait, or as a personalised being?

The original Greek does not help us because it can mean both. The word *tou ponerou* is either neutral or masculine and therefore in principle can mean either 'evil' or 'the evil one'. But modern scholars have noted that Mark and Luke use personal names like Satan or Beelzebub, so that when Matthew uses *tou ponerou* he is using it to name 'the evil one'. We can see this in the explanation of the parable of the sower where Matthew has 'the evil one comes and snatches away what is sown in the heart' (Matthew 13:19), Mark has 'Satan immediately comes and takes away the word that is sown in them' (Mark 4:15), and Luke has 'then the devil comes and takes away the word from their hearts', (Luke 8:12). Such usage has led scholars to conclude that the use in the Lord's Prayer is most likely also to indicate a personalised title – 'the evil one'.

The Bible has around 40 different ways of naming this being, from Beelzebul to the Prince of the World, from the Dragon to the Father of Lies. Most of them occur in the New Testament. We only have room here to consider a few. The identification of some of these figures with the devil was a later development.

This is true, for example, of the serpent that appeared in the Garden of Eden to tempt Adam and Eve. In the story itself (Genesis 3) the snake is simply that – a device for presenting temptation to Eve. The snake is itself one of God's creatures and is seen as wily and cunning. God's judgement upon the snake reflects its distinctive way of moving about, and the ancient belief that snakes flicking out their tongues was their way of eating the earth they travelled on. The judgement also indicates the relationship between snakes and human beings;

'Upon your belly you shall go,
and dust you shall eat
all the days of your life.
I will put enmity between you and the woman,
and between your offspring and hers;
he will strike your head,
and you will strike his heel.'

Genesis 3:14, 15

While it could be possible to see the story as an explanation of the dread people have of snakes and the ongoing danger snakes present, the account is clearly meant to convey much more than that. It is part of the biblical exploration of how evil entered into the world and its ever-present threat. Little wonder that Christian reflection saw here the start of that plight of humankind caught up in a struggle with evil that was doomed to continue unless God did something about it, as he did in the coming of Christ. It was this later reflection that identified the snake with the devil.

The Tempter figure appears again in the story of Job (Job 1–2). He appears as the Accuser within the heavenly court, where he is given God's permission to test Job's loyalty to God. It was in the Greek version of the Old Testament (the Septuagint) that he was called the devil (*ho diabolos*).

If God's whole creation was good, there is always the question as to how one of his good creatures came to be diabolical. The Old Testament itself does not give a clear answer to this question, but one passage in Isaiah was seen by early Christian scholars like Origen and Jerome to hold the clue. The passage comes in chapter 14. Taken as a whole, the chapter is clearly a 'taunt against the king of Babylon' (verse 4) in which it claims the king aspired to ascend to heaven and take a position above God (14:12-14). Such arrogance results in the king being 'brought down to Sheol, to the depths of the Pit' (verse 15). The title sarcastically ascribed to the king of Babylon in this passage is 'Day Star, son of Dawn'. The Latin translation of this is 'Lucifer', and at some point this passage was interpreted as an account of the rebellion of the angel Lucifer and his subsequent punishment. The moment of Lucifer's fall has been depicted in numerous religious paintings and was believed to have been referred to by Jesus in his response to the 70 returning from their mission: 'I watched Satan fall from heaven like a flash of lightening' (Luke 10:18).

The origin and the perpetuation of evil is thus associated with choice, and specifically the choice motivated by assertive and usurping pride. Adam and Eve chose the apple because they wanted to be as knowledgeable as God. Lucifer wanted to be above God. The creature rebelled against the creator, and the 'rebellion' continues. It resulted in a continuing battle played out in the lives of human beings and directed against God. It is a battle that Jesus took on. He himself was tempted by the devil in the wilderness, and his ministry of healing and exorcism was understood in terms of his fight against the devil. His opponents said he gained his power from the chief of the demons, Beelzebul (Mark 3:22), and Jesus pointed out the logical absurdity of such an accusation (Mark 3:23-6).

Some interpretations of Christ's work on the cross are expressed in terms of Jesus breaking the power of Satan (see Hebrews 2:14, 15). In the Book of Revelation, this struggle is seen to come to a conclusion in the final war led by Satan against Jesus, as a result of which Satan is cast into hell for all eternity, and heaven and earth are cleansed of all that is evil (Revelation 12:7-9; 20:7-10).

Satan

We have good reason, then, from the biblical evidence to say that in the Christian tradition evil is not some abstract force but is a 'personal being'. Religious art over the centuries, and especially in the Middle Ages, has tried to help us imagine what such a being might look like. The depictions emphasise what is horrific and repellent, to discourage us from following what is evil and warning us of the consequences of doing so. This fails, however, to capture the allure of evil. We are normally tempted not by what appals us but by what attracts us or is perceived to be attractive and desirable. Basic to the theological understanding of Satan is that he works through deception, tempting us through something that appears good but is actually wrong. St Paul told the Christians in Corinth that Satan 'disguises himself as an angel of light', as he warns them of false and deceitful ministers (2 Corinthians 11:13-15). The ultimate evil is to follow Satan as though he were God. The subtlety, deception and use of what is appealing make their appearance in the famous book by C. S. Lewis, *The Screwtape Letters*,[18] which

---

18. Harper Collins, 2001.

purport to be letters from a senior assistant of 'our Father below' to his novice tempter nephew.

In 1987, Pope John Paul II reaffirmed the Catholic belief in the devil:

> The devil is still alive and active in the world. The evil that surrounds us today, the disorders that plague our society, man's inconsistency and brokenness, are not only the results of original sin, but also the result of Satan's pervasive and dark action.[19]

Among evangelical leaders, 57 per cent have experienced or witnessed the devil or evil spirits being driven out of a person.[20]

Nevertheless, since the 1700s there has been a growing scepticism about the existence of a personal devil. American evangelical websites indicate that only a minority of the faithful believe in Satan, although there is a clear belief in the power of evil.

Whether we believe in a personal devil or not, there is no avoiding the reality of evil and its power that certainly feels very personal in the lives of individuals. Its destructive power manifests itself constantly, threatening our personal, social and national well-being. It surrounds us, sneaks up on us, entraps us and can overwhelm us. We catch a glimpse of just how appalling active evil can be when we see pictures of the ruins of hospitals, the faces of traumatised children and grieving parents in Mosul or Aleppo. Sadly, such horrors are not new. Jesus' prayer that asks God to deliver us from evil is as relevant now as it was then. Deliverance from the evil that distorts what is good. Deliverance from the evil that attracts and deceives. Deliverance from the evil that is hidden and the evil that confronts us.

If the main characteristic of evil is deceit, then the search for truth must play a very significant part in the way our own choices can partner God in the avoidance and escape from evil. While the devil is described

---

19. Spoken during a visit to the Sanctuary of Saint Michael the Archangel, 24 May 1987.
20. Global survey of Evangelical Protestant leaders, 2011. Available at www.pewforum.org (accessed 1 December 2016).

as the 'father of lies' (John 8:44), Jesus said of himself, 'I am the way, and the truth, and the life' (John 14:6). Deliverance from evil is not simply a matter of getting rid of what is wrong. Jesus showed that that can lead to a worse situation unless the gap is filled with what is good (Matthew 12:43-5). The prayer for deliverance from evil challenges us not only to seek to combat evil that overcomes the lives of others but also to fill their and our own lives with the life and love of Jesus, following in his way and learning from his truth.

PART B
Evil

The headmaster at my secondary school had a wife and two daughters. He was the only male in the house – apart from the cat, whom he called Cadbury. When asked why that name, he explained, 'He was 'born evil.'

Most people would agree that being evil is more a matter of nurture than nature, a characteristic you develop rather than are born with. We may have a general idea of what would lead us to say someone was evil, but being more specific is not so easy.

Who would you describe as being evil? Are there common elements in the way 'evil' people behave?

There has been a long tradition in Christianity and in other religions that explains the origins of evil through the action of a personal supernatural being and the influence that being has on the lives of men and women. For centuries it has been believed that it is possible for human beings to be 'possessed' by an evil spirit – whether that be the devil himself or one of his minions. All kinds of illnesses and mental disorders were explained in this way, and exorcism was the solution. There is generally a much greater caution these days around this whole area, and exorcism is usually seen as a last resort.

Spend a while reflecting on your own view of the nature of evil and how far you believe there is a personal force of evil. How do you understand evil in the context of a loving, holy God? What dangers can you see in a ministry of exorcism?

Suffering

Whether or not we believe in Satan or the devil, most people believe that evil exists. We only have to read the newspapers or watch the news on television. Alongside the most dramatic forms of evil there are myriad other events and actions that lead to suffering in our world. Our own lives may have been affected by a tragedy, and that may well have put our faith under considerable strain. As often as not it is not a matter of who deserves it and who doesn't. These things happen. Cancer can feel arbitrary, a natural disaster just comes 'out of the blue'. The young girl didn't deserve to be run over. It was an accident. It doesn't make such tragedies any easier either to understand or to cope with. In the midst of such events it is important not to feel guilt when things are not our fault. Too often people blame themselves for what is actually beyond their control. It takes considerable spiritual maturity to handle tragedy well.

A woman who had lost her young child through a mistake at a hospital felt that the whole experience was 'hellish' but had come through it with an amazing insight: 'It has shaped our lives since it happened but we have not allowed it to deform them.'

Think of someone you know who is facing tragedy. How might your prayers and your actions help their lives not to be deformed by it?

Thanksgiving

If our life has been relatively smooth sailing, it can be easy to assume that this is just how it should be rather than making it a source of thanksgiving. We can take good health for granted. Happiness is assumed to be a right. Having a loving family is not everyone's experience. Alongside a list of those whose suffering we bring to God in prayer, it is good to have a list of those specific things that make for a good life and for which we can give thanks.

How specific are your prayers of thanksgiving, or are they very general?

In including the request to God to keep us from evil, Jesus shows us that the loving Father to whom the whole of his prayer is addressed has an active concern for the well-being of each one of us. There is a mystery in the fact that evil still exists and our world is not free of suffering in spite of God being a loving Father. It is believed that in the cross and resurrection God showed once and for all that evil does not have the final say.

When we see people torn apart by the evil actions of others or suffering through illness or natural disaster, it is natural that we should pray to God to deliver them. We believe God hears us, but we do not always get the outcome we think should happen. Sometimes all that faith can do is hang on in trust, believing that in even the worst of situations God is present with us and with others.

In the face of suffering our prayers are sometimes a cry of anguish, and sometimes there can only be silence. There may be times when with Jesus we ask, 'My God, why have you forsaken me?' and hopefully we come through to say with Jesus, 'Into your hands I commend my spirit – my whole life.'

Doxology

In Matthew's Gospel the Lord's Prayer ends, in some of the ancient authorities, with a doxology:

> For the kingdom and the power and the glory are yours for ever. Amen.

It is generally agreed that this reflects liturgical use of the prayer in the early Church and is not original to the prayer Jesus gave us. Luke's Gospel does not have it.

It creates an appropriate conclusion, to some extent echoing thoughts in the opening section of the prayer: the kingdom we asked God to bring in, the power and glory which are part of that divine nature which is to be honoured, and the eternal nature of our heavenly Father.

So the prayer begins and ends with our thoughts directed to God, the one who meets our needs, forgives us our wrongs, and in whose love we find the strength to face whatever trials and tribulations we have to face. To him be glory. Amen

The Lord's Prayer, in the translation by Nicholas King

Our Father in heaven,
may your name be treated as holy;
may your kingdom come;
may your will be done, as in heaven,
(so) also on earth.
Give us today our bread for the coming day.
And let us off our debts,
just as we have let off all our debtors.
And don't bring us into temptation,
but deliver us from the Evil One.